ETCHINGS BY REMBRANDT *from the S. William Pelletier Collection*

ETCHINGS BY REMBRANDT

from the S. William Pelletier Collection

SUSAN DONAHUE KURETSKY

S. WILLIAM PELLETIER

FRANKLIN W. ROBINSON

ANDREW C. WEISLOGEL

HERBERT F. JOHNSON MUSEUM OF ART • CORNELL UNIVERSITY • ITHACA, NEW YORK • 2004

This catalogue accompanies an exhibition organized
by the Herbert F. Johnson Museum of Art at Cornell
University and presented at:

Herbert F. Johnson Museum of Art
Cornell University
Ithaca, New York
January 17 – April 4, 2004

Georgia Museum of Art
University of Georgia
Athens, Georgia
September 17 – November 14, 2004

This catalogue has been supported by a generous gift
from Genevieve and Richard Tucker.

The Institute of Museum and Library Services,
a federal agency that fosters innovation, leadership,
and a lifetime of learning, supports the operating
expenses of the Johnson Museum.

COVER:
Cornelis Claesz. Anslo, preacher (cat. no. 19), detail, enlarged.

INSIDE FRONT COVER:
The presentation in the temple with the angel: small plate
(cat. no. 3), detail, enlarged.

FRONTISPIECE:
Young man in a velvet cap: Petrus Sylvius (cat. no. 17)

INSIDE BACK COVER:
Cottages and farm buildings with a man sketching (cat. no. 25),
detail, enlarged.

BACK COVER:
Elderly couple behind a bank (cat. no. 5)

PUBLISHED BY:
Herbert F. Johnson Museum of Art
Cornell University
Ithaca, NY 14853
www.museum.cornell.edu

MUSEUM EDITOR:
Andrea Potochniak

TABLE OF CONTENTS

FOREWORD

It is an honor for the Herbert F. Johnson Museum to present the collection of Rembrandt's etchings assembled by Professor William Pelletier. Prof. Pelletier is known internationally as a distinguished scientist, teacher, and university administrator, but within the field of Dutch art, he is equally famous as both collector and scholar. This exhibition and catalogue are testimony to this second (or third) career. The Museum is privileged to present this superb group to its public, and to include Prof. Pelletier's brilliant essay in this publication. We are also grateful for the help of Prof. Pelletier's assistant, Cheryl Whiteford, for facilitating the exchange of information between Ithaca and Athens.

We are also most grateful to Professor Susan Donahue Kuretsky, Sara Gibson Blanding Professor of Art, Vassar College, for her essay, "Why Study Prints?" Her comments not only answer the title question but show us why she is both a highly respected scholar of Rembrandt's etchings and a revered teacher of them.

The curatorial work for this project has been done by Andrew Weislogel, and we are grateful to him for his hard work, attention to detail, and good humor, as well as for his excellent entries. Andrea Potochniak has helped edit this catalogue and has seen it through the press with her usual energy and skill. Registrar Matthew Conway and preparators Wil Millard, George Cannon, and David Ryan ably saw to the works' shipping and their installation. Undergraduate interns Lauren Butt, Sarah Burger, and Emily Bauman also provided invaluable support at various stages of the project. Gilbert Design Associates has once again designed an elegant publication.

We are especially grateful to William Eiland, director of the Georgia Museum of Art, University of Georgia, in Athens, as well as Romita Ray, curator of prints and drawings, and Patricia Miller, associate registrar at the GMOA, for their help at every stage, and for showing the works in their handsome galleries. Atlanta-based photographer Michael McKelvey provided the splendid reproductions found in this catalogue.

We are also very grateful to Genevieve and Richard Tucker for their support of this catalogue.
F.W.R.

Sheet with two studies:
a tree, and the upper part of a head of the artist wearing a velvet cap
(cat. no. 23), enlarged

I. There are perhaps two reasons why it is worth our while to look at Rembrandt today. First, he is like Shakespeare, who was born just forty-two years before him; he is interested in everything and everybody, from Old and New Testament subjects to scenes from ancient history, landscapes, cityscapes, animals, prominent contemporaries and people in the street, children, Jews, blacks, the rich, the poor, and beggars, and himself. He is the archetypal self-portraitist. It is a special privilege to experience this dynamic artist in this exhibition drawn from the Pelletier collection; these particular prints are unusually beautiful examples of Rembrandt's work.

The second reason why he is, I think, worth looking at is that he embodies Dutch art, Dutch culture itself, and seventeenth-century Dutch society is remarkably similar to American society today. In the 1600s, the Netherlands had just become independent from Spain; in fact, the Dutch were still in an eighty-year war of independence, ending in 1648. So this was a new country, with a relatively new language, new cities, and new prosperity; the Dutch were putting together a global commercial empire, trading silver for spices and many other commodities, as well as establishing trade routes that wound from the Baltic to the Mediterranean, from the Azores to South America, the Cape of Good Hope, Australia, Java, China, and India. For two hundred years, they were the only foreigners allowed to have any contact with Japan.

So the Netherlands was a dynamic country, and a very wealthy one. It was a republic; only in the nineteenth century did the Orange family become a royal family, instead of just leaders of the state. It was also a very urban society; agriculture became less and less important over the course of the century, and the other major industries – especially herring fishing, shipbuilding, and textiles, but also pottery and brickmaking – were not land-based. Perhaps most important, this was a middle-class society; the wealth and the political power were concentrated in the hands of the upper middle class, the regents, who lived in the crowded cities on or near the coast and the sea. The few aristocrats were tied to the land, and became less and less relevant as time went on. All of these factors created a demand for many, mostly small paintings (for homes with a number of small rooms), and for pictures of the world familiar to them – above all, landscapes, but also family portraits, still-lifes, and genre scenes – that is, scenes from everyday life, the market, the boudoir, and the tavern, with fewer and fewer religious scenes.

The society I have described, of course, could, in many ways, be our own: an urban, middle-class republic, affluent and, in many respects, increasingly secular.

For whatever reasons, Rembrandt is more than relevant today; he is almost as much a media icon as the Mona Lisa. Rembrandt's etchings are especially important because his use of the medium was new and highly experimental, and because these multiples were meant to be seen by a wide audience; he made so many etchings – close to three hundred – that he could not help revealing himself and his own emotions, from arrogance to self-pity and self-doubt, as well as his family and the world he encountered as he walked the streets of Amsterdam.

First, a brief word about the technique of etching, one of several print media. The artist, or his or her assistant, takes a copper plate and covers it with a thin layer of acid-resistant wax or resin. The artist then takes a needle and scratches it through that thin ground to make the intended design. Then the plate is put in an acid bath; the acid bites – or etches – into the copper where the needle has scratched the design. When the acid has bitten deeply enough into the plate, it is taken from the acid, the wax is removed, and thick, sticky ink is spread across the plate. The ink is then wiped off and stays only in the lines etched by the acid. A piece of paper is put on the plate, and paper and plate are put through a press; the pressure of the press forces the ink out of the etched lines and onto the paper, creating (in reverse) the design the artist intended. A good number of copies, or impressions, as they are called, can be taken from the plate, from fifty to a hundred or more, depending on various factors, before the lines begin to break down or become too shallow to hold the right amount of ink.

The genius of Rembrandt, especially when it comes to etchings, is that he combined his fascination with people and animals, and the stories of the Old and New Testament and ancient mythology, with an endless experimentation with the medium itself. The technique of etching was invented in Germany during the Renaissance, more than a century before Rembrandt, originally as a way of decorating armor; Rembrandt seems to have learned the classic technique of wax and acid and needle from another artist, Jan Joris van Vliet. However, he soon began to experiment; he would, for example, introduce drypoint and engraving lines into his etchings, that is, directly cutting into the plate, often throwing up curlicues of copper on either side of the line, called burr, which would catch the ink and make it broader and more velvety. He experimented with a sulphur tint, or, perhaps, a wax that was slightly porous, letting in some of the acid to bite into the plate, creating a film, or tone, on the paper. He experimented with different kinds of paper – vellum, or animal skin, Asian paper, paper of different colors, textures, and absorbency. This continual search for new effects is one reason why his work had such great impact on eighteenth- and nineteenth-century German, French, Italian, and Spanish artists. Goya, one of the giants of European art, consistently looked back to Rembrandt. He was a major influence on the French etching revival in the late nineteenth century, and he became a substitute for Picasso himself in many of the master's prints.

He even came to a new conception of the etching medium. This comes out, for example, in the various "mistakes" he made; in one of his etchings, the so-called "French bed," the woman has two left hands. He certainly noticed this, but he didn't bother to burnish one of them out. In his *Abraham Dismissing Hagar*, he etches in the beginning of a beam of a building, but he doesn't bother to finish it. In another case, he deliberately takes a plate by another artist, Hercules Seghers, burnishes out the right hand part of the image, and reworks that section with his engraving tool, the burin, to make an entirely new subject – producing a work that has the marks of two different artists, and two different styles, all in the same print.

In other words, he often treated the etching, which is a public medium, a multiple intended for the art market, as a drawing, which is usually a private medium, intended for the artist himself or herself. His prints are, therefore, amazingly spontaneous, seemingly unrehearsed, uncorrected. Both in his technique and in his subjects, which are so often himself or his family, he makes the private public; he opens himself up to everyone, and this, of course, makes him very "modern."

Another technical point worth mentioning here is the idea of the "state." Every time that an artist makes a change to his original plate, that is called a new state. Now and then, Rembrandt would produce only one state, the original composition, and print his whole edition from that. However, unlike most of his predecessors, he could make change after change, sometimes quite minor and sometimes major, rethinking the whole conception of the work. In other words, he tended to think of the etching plate as a kind of sketch pad, a place to think out loud, to reveal himself and his emotions, his obsessions – a sort of extended self-portrait, warts and all.

Interestingly, contrary to our Romantic idea of the neglected genius, Rembrandt was much admired – and widely collected – in his own lifetime, and throughout western Europe. There were collectors who insisted on buying not just every one of his etchings but every state of those etchings. Our twenty-first century fascination with this great artist is nothing new.

Eighty-one of Rembrandt's original plates survive and are now in various public and private collections. After the artist pulled fifty or seventy-five copies, or impressions, from the plate, he would sell it, and later owners of the plate were free to print their own editions from it, after Rembrandt's death. They often would recut certain details that might be getting paler due to excessive use or incompetent cleaning of the plate, thus creating new, posthumous states. In some cases, they would even cut the original plate into two or more pieces, and print editions from each of the pieces.

II. Rembrandt was born in the town of Leiden, known for its university and its textile factories, in 1606, and he died in Amsterdam in 1669, at age sixty-three. It is a moving experience to see this artist develop from his early twenties to his early sixties; it is a long journey, from a brash, brilliant "Generation Xer," self-confident and insecure at the same time, who wears his emotions on his sleeve, to someone more serene, his emotions under control and yet still intact inside him. We see him, over time, as someone both intimate and aloof, coolly appraising and open, powerful and fragile, but progressively that power is mixed with, and shadowed by, an awareness of pain, loss, and death. He is one of us.

Like all great artists, Rembrandt drew from many sources. One of his students, for example, worked in Persia, and it is perhaps from him that the master obtained a number of Persian miniatures, several of which he copied. He was particularly influenced by two artists, Lucas van Leiden and Jacques Callot. Lucas worked in the city of Leiden, as his name suggests, where Rembrandt himself grew up, and his best prints – engravings, in particular – were done in the early 1500s, when he was still in his teens. Lucas had a feeling for the homely details of everyday life that characterize so much of Rembrandt's work, as well as, on occasion, a monumentality and intensity of emotion that the later artist could reach.

Rembrandt's other major source is the early seventeenth-century French etcher, Jacques Callot. Callot, also, was an acute observer of daily life – like Rembrandt, he was especially fond of tramps and beggars as subjects – and he was remarkably sympathetic in his attitude toward the less fortunate in life. One of his greatest series is his *Miseries of War*, stunning images that have lost none of their force in our own century.

In an even deeper sense, Rembrandt was a creature of his own time and place. Even though it was invented early in the previous century, etching, one could argue, is a very baroque, seventeenth-century medium, in its immediacy, informality, and spontaneity, its freewheeling swirls of line which come from the greater freedom and ease of execution allowed by etching, as opposed to the more laborious engraving or woodcut, characteristics that must have appealed to the artist.

And one can see, over the thirty years or more of Rembrandt's etching activity, the profound change that seventeenth-century art as a whole went through, especially in the Netherlands; Rembrandt as a young man is imbued with the drama, even melodrama, of the High Baroque, whereas later his work is closer to what is sometimes called the Classical Baroque, simpler and more frontal, and parallel to the picture plane. Let's begin our detailed discussion of the artist's individual works with his portraits of people, including himself.

One of the most remarkable series of Rembrandt's etchings is his self-portraits. No other artist examined his own face more closely or more often. Aside from his natural interest in himself, the artist is using his face as a kind of laboratory of expressions, trying out pain, shock, surprise, and laughter (an emotion he was never comfortable with). In one print, he is, for example, frowning in a harsh light, his unruly hair curling up and around his head; in another, he is angry; and in a third he purses his mouth and starts back from us, shocked at what he sees. He can show himself, at age twenty-four, as a beggar, in rags, sitting at the side of the road, his hand out, or again, in a sheet of sketches, staring calmly out at us, young and self-contained, but surrounded by elderly peasants, sketched in at different angles of the sheet. Later on, in his thirties, he shows his wife, Saskia, sitting at the table behind him; his hat and his arm extend outward, surrounding and, in effect, protecting her. A few years later, he shows her in bed, dying.

Perhaps his most ambitious self-portrait etching is from 1639, when he was thirty-three years old. He has just seen in Amsterdam two great High Renaissance portraits by Titian and Raphael, and he models his pose on these Italian ideals from the previous century. Also, he wears a velvet cape, a gold chain, and a big beret, archaistic dress for the seventeenth century, but one more sign of his ambition to be considered equal to the masters of the Renaissance. And why shouldn't he think this? He's in his early thirties, he's already a great success in Amsterdam, the dynamic capital of a new, dynamic country, and he has married a wealthy aristocrat.

But even here, at the height of his powers, he cannot help seeing the dark side of his own personality: he squints nearsightedly out at us and frowns, his hair cascades, uncombed, out of his beret and down to his shoulders. He is not the ideal Renaissance gentleman, finally; he is somebody real, cocky and pretentious, emotional, unsure of himself.

His last etched self-portraits are in the late 1640s and early 1650s, when he is in his mid and late forties. He confronts himself, head on, with no fancy dress and no pretentious poses or expressions; he is simply recording what he sees, and what he sees is a face not too different from what we see, when we look in the mirror. Or, as he did more than twenty years earlier, he presents himself as just one among a sheet of sketches; the other figures are, as before, peasants and beggars.

The range of the people who interested Rembrandt is remarkable. A blind fiddler, guided by his dog, moves slowly across the page; a man urinates in public; a woman, who has no home of her own, squats by the side of the road and relieves herself. Or, a few years later, a beggar family stops at a door; the older man, who is blind, plays a hurdy-gurdy, and the mother extends her hand to the householder at the half door, well-protected by massive walls and even bars, as he gives her a coin. Rembrandt carefully documents the boy's clothing, his hat and jacket, the water jug, and his stockings, one of which has fallen down. It is a quiet, even beatific moment – an act of charity, the rich and secure helping the homeless and vulnerable.

At the same time that he shows peasants and beggars and members of the class of homeless vagrants and outsiders called the *grauw*, he makes portraits of the power elite: the aristocrat Jan Six in his study, reading, perhaps, one of his own plays; Arnold Tholinx, the inspector of medical colleges in Amsterdam, a rather forbidding figure, with his expressionless face and dueling scar on his left cheek; the much more congenial figure of Jan Lutma, a fellow artist and the most prominent and successful silversmith in Amsterdam; the extraordinary posthumous image of Jan Sylvius, a Dutch Reformed preacher, reaching out to us from beyond the grave through a trompe-l'oeil "porthole"; and Ephraim Bonus, a Jewish physician, caught in a subtle web of lines, a shifting sea of tones of gray in a simple interior. Although Rembrandt was a Protestant, he was fascinated by the Jews of Amsterdam; he lived near the Jewish ghetto, and illustrated a book of mysticism by Menasseh Ben Israel, and he used Jews as models for his figures of Christ, an interesting attempt at historical accuracy.

Like Shakespeare, however, he looked at everything and was interested in everything: a hog tied up for slaughter, being made fun of by three little children, a print in the Pelletier collection; a rat catcher, a raffish figure who not only kills rats but keeps them as pets, as the householder at the half door turns away in disgust; a pancake woman, surrounded by hungry children (and a hungry dog); a couple making love; and nudes, everything from a fat, overblown naked woman grinning out at us to a woman in profile, next to a stove, or turning away from us, into the darkness. He is also very

Cat. no. 24

interested in sex, and he doesn't hesitate to show couples making love. In his "French bed," with that extra left hand, he indulges in a visual pun: a soft hat with a feather, on an upright bedpost. A large feather on a hat was a symbol of sexual desire in the seventeenth century. He also shows a monk making love in a wheat field with what seems to be a jug nearby, making the image into a vaguely anti-Catholic reference to holy communion, as it were. Rembrandt is even interested in men who reject sex, and several times he depicts the Old Testament subject of Joseph fleeing the advances of Potiphar's wife. A particularly moving work shows Jupiter as an old satyr pulling the bedclothes away from a luxurious sleeping nude, an etching made when Rembrandt himself was in his fifties. Interestingly, in 1936, when Picasso is in his fifties, he too shows a satyr gently lifting a sheet from a sleeping naked woman.

Beginning in the 1640s, when he is in his mid thirties, he adds a whole new category to his repertoire: the landscape. Who knows why he takes up this subject? Perhaps it is simply because landscape was by far the most popular subject of Dutch artists, and he is responding to that. The horizontal format may also have appealed to him, with the flat Dutch landscape and high sky that hints at a new phase of Dutch art, more classical in some ways and less High Baroque. Whatever the reason, he begins to take walks in the countryside around Amsterdam.

Sometimes, the etchings show the familiar skyline of windmills and churches of the capital city; his most famous landscape etching juxtaposes three trees, silhouetted against the sky, and the city far in the left background. The sky here is especially dramatic, with slashing straight lines of rain in the upper left cutting across twisting towers of clouds behind them, giving way to bright, sunlit sky on the right. In the left foreground, an older couple sits and fishes, while on the right, a younger man and woman make love in a bower of bushes beneath the dike. Other landscapes are even more relaxed and homier; a flock of sheep, for example, crowds a country road, while a horse rolls in the field to the right, and trees and barns huddle close to the ground behind.

III.   Perhaps Rembrandt's profoundest etchings are of religious subjects, from the Old and New Testament. He is a master storyteller and is able to convey narrative and a whole range of human emotions on a small scale, on these little sheets of paper. And he always has his own take on these stories, which were so familiar to everyone in the seventeenth century. For example, in the parable of the Good Samaritan, who has rescued a poor wayfarer attacked by bandits and brought him to a wayside inn, incredibly, the diagonal that is the basis of the composition begins, in the lower right, with a dog defecating in our faces. In another etching, the angel appears to the shepherds, announcing Christ's birth, and all the players – shepherds, cows, sheep – fall all over themselves in shock and surprise, and even the trees twist and turn. To turn to the Old Testament, Rembrandt presents Abraham casting out Hagar and Ishmael, one of the favorite subjects of artists in the seventeenth century, who delighted in showing the righteous anger of the Old Testament prophet dismissing from his house his mistress and bastard son.

Rembrandt, however, has his own view of this violent and disturbing story. He presents Abraham as literally torn between his two families. His right hand and right foot turn toward Sarah in the window and little Isaac peering slyly around the Dutch half door, while his left hand and left foot reach out toward Hagar and Ishmael. Rembrandt loved fat women; Sarah is thin and gaunt, while Hagar is plump, with a double chin. And how do you show a child being cast out of his own home by his own father? Perhaps the most eloquent way is to show him from behind, his face turned away from us.

Even the story of Adam and Eve is not immune from the artist's individual point of view – and his humor. Here Rembrandt and Saskia themselves, newly married, are presented not as ideal nudes but as naked and fat, warts and all; even the elephant in the background seems to be making a comment on Saskia's ample proportions.

These are all early works, from his twenties and early thirties. Later, in his forties and early fifties, a different spirit pervades these subjects. For example, one of his most famous etchings is the "Hundred Guilder Print," represented in the Pelletier collection. A guilder in the seventeenth century is about what a skilled artisan, a carpenter or fisherman, would earn in a day; the average annual income was about 300 guilders. So a hundred guilders was a hefty, even famous price for a print, a multiple of which he seems to have made perhaps fifty or seventy-five impressions.

Cat. no. 27

We see here a remarkable scene: Christ receiving, from the right, the sick and the lame, and from the left, children and babes in arms. He is, however, among his enemies; the fat and affluent burghers on the far left turn away from him, in their skepticism, and he is depicted outside the city walls, as the true outsider that he is. Even the three animals – camel, donkey, and dog – turn away from him; lacking souls, they cannot participate in his miracle. In the foreground are a shell, a symbol of the pilgrim, just in front of the kneeling woman, and, to the left, a flowering branch, hope for the future, reaching out of a depression in the ground.

This elegiac mood appears fairly often in these late religious subjects. For example, in 1654, he does a series of six small plates of the childhood of Christ, showing the shepherds in the stable, the circumcision, the flight into Egypt, the

Holy Family with the cat, Christ in the temple disputing with the doctors, and the return from the temple. The etching of the circumcision, also represented superbly in the Pelletier collection, is particularly beautiful; it is one of the few times that this ritual is shown in the stable, instead of the temple, its traditional place. The stable emphasizes Christ's humble beginnings. Even more remarkable is the ladder leaning against a pole on the left; this is a reference to the Crucifixion, the last pain of Christ, present here at the scene of his first ritual pain.

Three of Rembrandt's children die before their first birthday, and a fourth, the famous Titus, dies in his late twenties. Throughout his life, the artist returns to the theme of father and son, and especially Abraham and his troubled relationship with his two sons, Ishmael and Isaac. We have already discussed his etching of 1637 of Abraham dismissing Hagar and Ishmael into the wilderness, where his son will become a perpetual wanderer – we remember the first line of *Moby Dick*: "Call me Ishmael."

One of his most powerful prints shows a later episode in the story of Abraham. The Lord has told Abraham to take Isaac, his one remaining son and heir, up to the top of a mountain and sacrifice him. Here we see the climactic moment of this dramatic, disturbing, inexplicable story; Abraham covers Isaac's eyes, exposing his vulnerable throat, and is about to kill him. However, just now, the angel of the Lord descends and prevents him from making this sacrifice. The angel's pose is not overtly dramatic, as it was in Rembrandt's earlier, youthful depictions of this scene. Rather, he descends in a tunnel of heavenly light and firmly, but gently, lovingly, embraces the prophet. On the left side of the print under the angel's right wing we can see the hindquarters of the ram, his horns caught in the bushes; he will soon be sacrificed in place of Isaac.

Let us end with two of his greatest plates: *Christ Presented to the People*, and the *Three Crosses*, both from the 1650s. Rembrandt had addressed the subject of Christ presented to the people twenty years before, in a highly baroque work of 1636. Here, a convex curve of figures streams out toward us and then recedes into the crowd behind; a forest of spears clusters around Christ's head, as young and old press forward, gesture, argue, and show their weapons. In the far left stands a column with a statue of the Roman emperor on top, looking suspiciously like the reigning head of the Dutch state, Frederick Henry, in Rembrandt's own time.

When the artist returns to this subject twenty years later, in 1655, he keeps many of the same elements: the crowd, the soldiers, the cruelty, indifference, and disputes, the bewilderment of Pilate – but the whole mood has changed. There is no convex stream of people surging toward us, but a massive building, symmetrical, with its main platform parallel to the picture plane and the crowd of figures ranged around it and almost dwarfed by it. A mother plays with a child; another child peers around the corner at the drama; a woman watches quietly from a window. A young fellow with a feathered hat, who looks like the young Rembrandt, gestures on the left, as an evil Boschian old man whispers in his ear. St. Peter is isolated on the right, watching in consternation, and Pilate's hand is in the dead center of the composition, offering Christ and asking the crowd for its decision.

Perhaps the high point of Rembrandt's printmaking is reached in his *Three Crosses*. Every time an artist makes a change on the copper plate, as we mentioned before, it is called a new state. Sometimes, these changes are minor, of interest mainly to the specialist. In this case, however, the changes in state are dramatic, and they transform the whole image. The early states of the *Three Crosses*, from 1653, present the drama of Christ's death among a crowd of figures; the kneeling centurion on the left, converted in this final moment, is balanced by the women on the right, clustered around the grieving Virgin. St. John tears at his hair above her, while other figures – believers, turbaned Orientals, soldiers – come and go all around them, as the sacred light from above cascades down, cutting through the enveloping darkness at noon.

Extraordinary as this image is, it pales next to the following state, the fourth. Now, Rembrandt has rethought the whole plate and plowed into it with his drypoint tool, throwing up thick burr, or curlicues of copper on either side of the lines, which catch the ink and make a wonderfully thick, velvety line. All the elements from the earlier state are still here – the three crosses, the soldiers, John and the Virgin Mary, but they are now transformed, isolated in a kind of silent nightmare. Above all, the play of light and shadow has taken on even greater meaning; light and shadow have become virtually three-dimensional, tangible objects, black shadows emanate from Christ, and light falls from above like sheets of ice or glass. The ghosts of the figures in the earlier states move almost invisibly underneath the dark, heavy lines of this state, creating a feeling of tension and unease throughout the composition. The gestures of the few figures we see clearly become simple and emblematic, filled with meaning. The whole image is one of pain and revelation, and redemption.

Here then is an artist Shakespearean in his range and ambition, in the power of his self-assertion as well as the power of his empathy, whether beggars by the side of the road or hogs waiting to be slaughtered or his dying wife. He is fascinated by the old and the young, by prominent Dutch burgers and Jewish physicians, by the landscape around Amsterdam, and by scenes from the Old and New Testament. His prints have the energy and vividness and presence of life itself, and this is why we look at him still, three and a half centuries later.

Franklin W. Robinson
The Richard J. Schwartz Director
Herbert F. Johnson Museum of Art

Joseph's Coat Brought to Jacob
(cat. no. 12), detail, enlarged

Rembrandt van Rijn: A Selection of His Etchings

Among the great spectrum of personalities in the history of art, Rembrandt Harmensz. van Rijn emerges as one of the geniuses who have forged their own styles and stamped their own influence on posterity. In his etched work in particular, Rembrandt's unique position is realized to an even greater extent than in his paintings.[1]

Among etchers there was no one who combined the same control and mastery of the medium with a fraction of Rembrandt's significance of expression. In his own day his etchings attracted the attention of collectors and fellow artists. The Sicilian collector Don Antonio Ruffo, in 1669, requested and purchased a group of one hundred eighty-nine Rembrandt etchings. In his 1662 book, *Sculptura*, John Evelyn's (1620–1706) comment, "the incomparable Rembrandt, whose etchings and engravings are of a particular spirit," stimulated a strong interest in Rembrandt's prints by Britons. Thus Richard Maitland, fourth Earl of Lauderdale, in 1689, offered at auction his collection of "Rembrandt's Complete Work, 420 figures." A perhaps even finer group of Rembrandt etchings was assembled by his Dutch contemporary, the Amsterdam dealer Jan Pietersz. Zomer (1641–1724), who described his three albums of Rembrandt etchings as "complete, including every state, excellent impressions."[2] Today, over three hundred years later, connoisseurs pay sums in the six and even seven figures for fine impressions of certain Rembrandt etchings.

As a background, a sketch of Rembrandt's early life may be helpful. He was born in Leiden, the ninth of ten children, on July 15, 1606, to Harmen Gerritszoon van Rijn, a prosperous Leiden miller, and Neeltgen Willemsdr. van Zuytbrouck, a baker's daughter.[3] His parents enrolled him, on May 20, 1620, as a student at the University of Leiden, but after a few months he decided he was not suited to academic learning and left the University to study painting.[4] His first teacher was Jacob van Swanenburgh, a local painter of architecture, under whom he worked for about three years during the period from 1621 to 1624. Later he studied for six months in Pieter Lastman's studio in Amsterdam and possibly also with Jacob Pynas. About 1625 he set up as an independent artist in Leiden, probably sharing a studio with his friend Jan Lievens. The first painting identified as by Rembrandt is dated 1625. In the autumn of 1631, he settled in Amsterdam, living with the art dealer Hendrick van Uylenburgh. Rembrandt received his first important commission in 1632 – the group portrait of *Dr. Tulp, Giving a Lesson on Anatomy* (Bredius[5] 403; The Hague, Mauritshuis). In 1634 he married Saskia van Uylenburgh, his social superior, and the niece of Hendrick van Uylenburgh. He became, until about 1642, the most successful portrait painter in the city. He then was able to lead the life of a great bourgeois painter, and, like Rubens, he conducted the business of a large workshop.

Rembrandt's etchings[6] may be divided into three periods, each of which possesses predominant characteristics. In the first, between about 1626 and 1639, the pure etched line is the commonest medium and his draftsmanship is characterized by carefulness and even timidity.[7]

In the second or middle period from 1640 to 1650, Rembrandt is more concerned with the tone of his compositions than with their outward design. Work with the drypoint[8], a process involving scratching the copper plate with a sharp needle rather than biting the copper in an acid bath, became important in his style; we see frequent use of the drypoint in emphasizing the effects of light and shadow.

In the third period, from 1651 until 1665, the vigor and the breadth of his handling is enhanced. The forms are less conventional, the lines of shading are openly spaced, and the touch is more certain and spontaneous and less evidently conscious. He uses drypoint with the full effect of the burr as much as etching. Chiaroscuro, the interplay between light and shadow, now becomes of great importance. Though occasionally still rendered in some plates by closely hatched shading, the chiaroscuro is often achieved by a quicker method which relies on the variations obtainable by means of a thin film of ink left on the surface of the plate during printing.[9] Again and again he introduced modulations by varying his printing technique as he experimented with various kinds and qualities of papers.

To appreciate Rembrandt's etchings his earliest trials or experiments must be considered. Though he became a great artist, yet he had to learn by slow and tedious experiments, particularly in his early years. His first dated etchings are of 1628. Today, however, after considerable debate, many scholars, such as Karel G. Boon, George Biörklund, Ludwig Münz, Seymour Slive, and Christopher White, agree that Rembrandt had already begun to etch before 1628 and believe that *The Circumcision* (Gersaint[10] 48; Seidlitz[11] 398; White-Boon[12] S. 398) of about 1626 is among his very first attempts.[13] Works of this kind belong to his initial gropings. When he made such prints as these, he had only recently left Pieter Lastman's studio. Rembrandt here tried to create a lively sketch.[14] With all the shortcomings of the execution, his composition here represents a step forward. Nowhere previously had *The Circumcision* been represented with such tense immediacy as a scene glimpsed purely accidentally. Rembrandt's entirely new approach transforms *The Circumcision* from a cult picture into one in which we as spectators share in the passion of Christ. Notice, for example, the spectators above, or the man putting on his spectacles so as to better see what is happening to the crying child. Figures such as these taken singly had been used earlier, "but nowhere had there been this range of feeling, varying from the curiosity of the onlookers to the pain and foreboding in the face of the Virgin...how close is the connection created between the spectator and the Child, whom the spectator sees over the shoulder of the bending priest."[15] This print clearly predicts Rembrandt's great gift for sensing a symbolic situation as a reality charged with individual human emotion. At this time Rembrandt's etchings were intended only as sketches in which he sought to express the character of the subject matter at hand.

Rembrandt did another such subject, *The Circumcision: Small Plate* (Bartsch[16] 48), of about 1630 with the main group derived from an engraving by Hendrik Goltzius (B. 18). Rembrandt has added his personal interpretation to this traditional scene – a loudly crying infant surrounded by a richly robed priest and monumental architecture. This rare and early impression shows burr on the mouth, along the head and the right shoulder, arm and hand of the Christ child. Noticeable burr is also

Cat. no. 1

Cat. no. 4

on the top of the hat of the priest standing at the left and along the head and right shoulder of the priest who holds the Christ child.

After his return from Lastman's studio in 1625, Rembrandt lived quietly with his family. From his paintings we know that his mother and father, his eldest brother Adriaen, and his younger sister Lysbeth sat as models for him. From his earliest etchings it is apparent how lovingly he viewed his own familiar surroundings. In 1628 he made two etchings of his mother, one in a fine diffused light, *The Artist's Mother, Head and Bust: Three Quarters Right* (B. 354), with the skin texture and hair characterized with great subtlety and precision. He pictures his mother with a warm, inward-turning gaze and tender thoughts suffusing her face. He records her every wrinkle with incomparable delicacy.[17] The effective dark printing around the jaw gives a rounded, sculptured quality to the old woman's head.[18] This is a magnificent and very successful work. Rembrandt does not achieve the same perfection for many years afterward, yet it lacks some of the solidity and technical economy of his mature etchings.[19] Its wonderful sympathy and close observation give us a foretaste of what Rembrandt's talent would afterward lead to.

This impression is a previously unrecorded state[20], intermediate between the first and second, i.e., the face and bust have been completed as in the second state, but before the copper plate was trimmed to a regular rectangle. There is burr in many areas of the plate, for example on the long hairs extending from the right side of the woman's head and on the reversed "L" in the lower right corner of the plate.

The Artist's Mother in a Cloth Headdress, Looking Down: Head Only (B. 351) was done a few years later, in 1633. This very rare and richly printed etching is a little jewel and a worthy companion to the 1628 etched portrait.

At this period Rembrandt took growing pleasure in the distinctive characteristics of the etching medium. From it he obtained effects impossible from any other technique; the velvet dark tones in deep shadow, the transparent halftones, or the delicate, tender lines vibrating with liveliness are impossible in either engraving or drawing. The relief or slightly elevated character of the etched line contributes to these unique qualities.[21]

Rembrandt was fascinated by the scenes that surrounded him in the street, especially the beggars and street characters (rat-poison vendors, musicians, quacksalvers, tramps) that were part of life in the cities of northern Holland. He made more than twenty etchings of beggars, many during his years in Leiden.[22] Rembrandt's reasons for creating so many etchings of beggars can only be conjectured. Some scholars have interpreted the series as a commentary on social injustice and a gesture of Rembrandt's solidarity with the very poor. J. P. Filedt Kok regards this attitude as simply a projection of nineteenth- and twentieth-century attitudes into the past.[23] The inspiration for these works was likely Jacques Callot's series of *Les Gueux* of 1622 (Lieure[24] 479–503). Rembrandt sought to capture the general appearance of the various street types. Richard Godfrey's comments about Rembrandt's etchings of beggars are appropriate here:

> Likewise Rembrandt's beggars…are in marked contrast to the chic peasants of Bloemaert's drawing manuals….His little portraits crackle with animation when placed beside the rows of engraved portraits by Delff after Mierevelt, motionless in their cartwheel ruffs and starched clothes, lending respectability to walls in many Dutch houses.[25]

In the *Elderly Couple behind a Bank* (B. 165) of about 1630, the couple's expression is eloquent of human misery. Their mouths are open and their features are distorted by piercing laments of their unhappiness. Note how effectively the savage,

Cat. no. 2

Cat. no. 11

Cat. no. 5

hungry look of the old woman is expressed. The lines are clearly bitten, and in order to depict the darker contrast of the bank, from which the couple emerges, he has added more deeply bitten shading. This very fine impression is of the extremely rare fourth state of nine.

Cat. no. 6 One of the finest of his early etchings of beggars is *Man in a Coat and Fur Cap Leaning against a Bank* (B. 151) of about 1630. This vivid and masterly sketch was done during Rembrandt's early period in Leiden. In this etching he has achieved a more coherent sense of space, volume, and mass than in the *Elderly Couple behind a Bank* (B. 165).[26]

The impression is an exceptionally early one of the first state of three. There is drypoint burr on the man's beard and on the monogram in the upper right corner, indicating Rembrandt scratched his signature directly onto the plate.

Cat. no. 7 Many of Rembrandt's early etchings of genre are executed with an exquisitely delicate needle. *Peasant with His Hands behind His Back* (B. 135) of 1631 is a charming example, printed with plate tone and possessing generous margins. Rather loose in treatment, its spontaneity gives us a realistic view of a peasant that Rembrandt may have encountered in life. About this time he did several miniature studies of men's heads, such as the extremely *Cat. no. 8* rare *Head of a Man in a High Cap* (B. 302) and *Cat. no. 9* *Grotesque Profile: Man in a High Cap* (B. 326).

Cat. no. 29 A later peasant study is the lightly drawn *Peasant Family on the Tramp* (B. 131) of about 1652. The rare, first state shown here exhibits false biting on the left edge of the man's hat, on the upturned bill of his hat, on the back pack, and on his belt. These areas of false biting were corrected in the second state. There are traces of an earlier etching of an old man at the lower right, adjacent to the peasant's staff.

Cat. no. 3 In 1630 Rembrandt did the earliest rendition of *The Presentation in the Temple with the Angel: Small Plate* (B. 51), a subject he returned to twice more: in 1640 with a large, unresolved composition (B. 49), and again in the 1650s with his great *Presentation in the Dark Manner* (B. 50).

In accordance with Mosaic Law, Joseph and Mary presented their firstborn son in the Jerusalem Temple. The aged Simeon, to whom it had been revealed that he would see the Redeemer before his death, recognizes the Child and offers praise to the Lord. Anna, a prophetess, also recognizes the Christ child.[27]

In this small print Rembrandt has positioned the figures in a majestic architectural space with the key figures in a closely packed group in the center. The angel pointing out the Christ child to Anna is an unusual iconographical detail.[28] This print is related to the painting of *Simeon in the Temple* (Bredius 543; The Hague) of 1630 in its composition, the figures, and their clothing.[29]

Only two impressions of the uncut first state are recorded, in Amsterdam and London; this impression was probably pulled shortly after the plate was reduced in size. It possesses all the signs of being very early, with sharp plate edges and an impressive depth of tone for a pure etching of this early period. The bright, unpressed sheet with its large margins reinforces the impact of this print.[30]

From 1633 to 1635 Rembrandt passed through a critical period that led to many Biblical etchings. *Joseph's Coat Brought to Jacob* (B. 38) of about 1633 *Cat. no. 12* illustrates the Old Testament story[31] of the young Joseph who was seized by his jealous brothers and sold to Ishmaelite merchants as a slave. To disguise this act the brothers slaughtered a goat and dipped Joseph's coat in the blood. Later they took the coat to their father Jacob and told him they had found it. Jacob recognized the coat, concluded a wild animal had devoured Joseph, and was overcome with grief. The fine descriptive line and dramatic use of multiple bitings mark this as a work of the early 1630s, usually assigned to about 1633.

This brilliant, early impression of the first state of two shows drypoint burr on the sleeve and cuff of the pointing man and also a second faint outline of his thumb, below and longer than the upper one, a feature that disappears in later impressions.

Cat. no. 15

The Tribute Money (B. 68) dates from about 1635. This is a superb and rich impression of the first state of two with burr on the back of the standing man at the left. The etching is an illustration of the incident recorded in the Gospel of Matthew, in which the Pharisees attempt to trap Christ by a trick question into a response on which they could base a charge of disloyalty to the Roman government:

> Then the Pharisees went and plotted how to entangle him in his talk. And they sent their disciples to him, along with the Herodians, saying "Teacher, we know that you are true and teach the way of God truthfully and you do not care about anyone's opinion, for you are not swayed by appearances. Tell us, then, what you think. Is it lawful to pay taxes to Caesar or not?" But Jesus, aware of their malice, said, "Why put me to the test, you hypocrites? Show me the coin for the tax." And they brought him a denarius. And Jesus said to them, "Whose likeness and inscription is this?" They said, "Caesar's." Then he said to them, "Therefore render to Caesar the things that are Caesar's, and to God the things that are God's."[32]

The individual expressions on the faces of the Pharisees are brilliantly delineated – showing them confounded by Christ's reply.

A print of very high quality is *The Stoning of St. Stephen* (B. 97) of 1635. Chapter 7 of the Acts of the Apostles describes how Stephen was driven out of the city and stoned for spreading the gospel of Christ, thus becoming the first Christian martyr. Rembrandt had painted this subject ten years before (Bredius 531A; Lyons), but in this etching he changed from a horizontal to a vertical composition and eliminated many of the figures to focus on the central, violent act of martyrdom.[33] The

Cat. no. 14

print illustrated is a brilliant, early, lightly toned impression of the first state of two. It shows burr on the black spot above Stephen's shoe, on the sash to the right of his head, along the nose of the man holding Stephen's robe and on Stephen's right heel. In the white area above and to the right of his slipper there are fine, vertical polishing scratches that extend up into the lower part of Stephen's robe and to the right of the robe, features indicative of a very early impression.

Christ Driving the Money Changers from the Temple (B. 69), inscribed: *Rembrandt f. 1635*, was my first Rembrandt acquisition. The New Testament records two occasions when Christ drove the money changers from the temple, one at the beginning of his ministry (John 2:13–17) and one near the end (Matthew 21:12–13). The etching seems to follow the text in John most closely:

Cat. no. 13

> The Passover of the Jews was at hand and Jesus went up to Jerusalem. In the temple he found those who were selling oxen and sheep and pigeons, and the money changers sitting there. And making a whip of cords, he drove them all out of the temple, with the sheep and oxen. And he poured out the coins of the money changers and overturned their tables. And he told those who sold the pigeons, "Take these things away; do not make my Father's house a house of trade."

In this print, a brilliant second state of two, not Christ's face, but his hand and whip are placed in the strongest light. He follows closely here the example of Albrecht Dürer in the *Small Passion* (B. 23) woodcut series.[34] This etching exemplifies the foreign influence on Rembrandt's work. Beside the figure of Christ borrowed from Dürer, a Venetian influence is evident.

In contrast to some of Rembrandt's large plates is the tiny *Polander Standing with Arms Folded* (B. 140), also of about 1635. Despite the traditional title, the man is seen to be playing a barrel organ that he holds with his left arm and supports with his left leg. In style and theme this print

Cat. no. 16

belongs to the group of beggars and street types discussed earlier. This delicate, masterful little gem is extremely rare and shows how much Rembrandt could accomplish with a very few well-placed strokes.

Cat. no. 17 In 1637 he produced an especially effective plate, the *Young Man in a Velvet Cap* (B. 268), identified by F. Schmidt-Degener[35] in 1932 as Rembrandt's student, Ferdinand Bol. D. de Hoop Scheffer of the Rijksmuseum, Amsterdam, has now convincingly identified the subject as Petrus Sylvius because his name is inscribed on the verso of this early impression in a seventeenth-century hand.[36] Petrus Sylvius was the son of Pastor Jan Cornelis Sylvius, whose portrait was twice etched by Rembrandt (B. 266 and 280) and who was the uncle and guardian of Rembrandt's wife, Saskia. Rembrandt's close ties to the Sylvius family give credence to the execution of a portrait of the young theological scholar, seated in his study with his pile of books.

In describing this impression the editors of the Ritman catalogue wrote:

> This impression is rich, printed with tone and so early that it seems almost to have burr, even though no drypoint has been used. It must be one of the very first pulls…. The richness of the impression is shown off to added advantage by the wide proportionate margins and total absence of damage or evidence of cleaning.[37]

The *Young Man in a Velvet Cap* is an impressive piece both in design and in strong, simple execution. It suggests a memory of a portrait by Hans Holbein and represents a great advance on his early prints. This plate is reminiscent in its high quality of the early portrait of *The Artist's Mother* (B. 354) of 1628.

> The firmness and exquisite sobriety of the handling in this plate entitle it to rank among Rembrandt's masterpieces. It is impossible to forget the depth of expression in the sitter's melancholy face, his mournful eyes and suffering look,

his air of weakness and ill health…. Taking into account the extreme simplicity of the execution it seems…that expressive power could hardly go further.[38]

In the firmness of touch and its expressive yet restrained quality, this etching has never failed to appeal to artists. For example, the young Edgar Degas, learning his craft, in emulation of Rembrandt's *Young Man*, etched in 1857, a self-portrait, *Edgar Degas, par lui-même*,[39] the melancholy introspection of which has left its mark on many Degas portraits of similarly brooding nature.[40, 41] About 1860, Degas also etched in reverse a copy of Rembrandt's *Young Man* (*Jeune homme assis et réfléchissant d'après Rembrandt van Rijn;* Delteil no. 13).

Cat. no. 18 Rembrandt etched, in 1638, an exquisite little plate, *Joseph Telling His Dreams* (B. 37). Joseph, his father's favorite, has just told two dreams which indicate that his brothers would one day make obeisance to him.[42] The brothers' unhappy reactions are depicted with vigor and conviction. In this plate Rembrandt is attempting an elaborate study of human character. The print contains a wealth of character study in the heads of the envious brothers.[43] Arnold Houbraken[44] recounts that even in Rembrandt's lifetime ardent enthusiasts sought to possess this print in two states, with the white (as here, state ii) and the shaded (state iii) faces.

The etchings of 1639 to 1645 reveal that a change in Rembrandt's vision of the outside world had started even before the personal calamities which are usually considered the underlying cause of his change of style. We know that his mother died in 1640. Then, in 1642, his wife Saskia passed away. Each of these deaths exerted a powerful, sobering influence on Rembrandt.[45] During this period he began to turn his attention to landscape – perhaps as a means of solace.

Cat. no. 25 *Cottage and Farm Buildings with a Man Sketching* (B. 219) of about 1641–1643 is a freely drawn sketch of a dilapidated farmhouse of the type

Rembrandt knew and often drew, the *langhuisstolp* – a combination of the two main types around Amsterdam, the essentially longitudinal *langhuis* (long house) and the square *stolp*.[46] This print is one of three landscapes, all dating from the 1640s, in which Rembrandt included an artist. The other two are *The Three Trees* (B. 212) and the drawing, *View of Diemen, with a man seated in foreground, drawing* (Benesch [47] 838).

Cat. no. 26   A small, delicate landscape is *The Shepherd and His Family* (B. 220), dated 1644. Rembrandt etched this subject on a plate which had not been cleaned, for the print is covered with scratches among which one can see the outlines of two circles, one in the center and another higher up, perhaps the remains of a previous etching. The sunlight and air, the flock of sheep and goats and the hill in the distance crowned with romantic buildings are close in feeling to Claude Lorrain's etchings of ideal landscapes of almost the same date and with which Rembrandt may have been familiar.[48]

According to the account in the eleventh chapter of the Gospel of John, when Jesus heard that his friend Lazarus, the brother of Mary and Martha, had died, he went to Bethany, and restored to life the man who had been dead four days. Jesus ordered that the stone be removed from the mouth of the cave tomb. Martha protested, saying: "Lord, by this time there will be an odor, for he has been dead four days."[49] Jesus answered: "Did I not tell you that if you believed you would see the glory of God?"[50] After removal of the stone and a brief prayer, Jesus called in a loud voice: "Lazarus, come out."[51] It is this moment, as Lazarus awakens from death, that Rembrandt has chosen to illustrate in this small etching, *The Rais-*
Cat. no. 20   *ing of Lazarus: Small Plate* (B. 72) of 1642, shown in a rich, early first state of two.

This beautifully composed etching pictures the tomb in the near foreground, with Jesus and the spectators assembled at the left. The scene is inside a cave with a lightly sketched vista of a tower on a hill, visible through the cave opening. A regular system of cross-hatching is employed to depict the dark cave shadows that surround the figures so that they are absorbed into the landscape. Areas of cross-hatching are juxtaposed to suggest the play of light on the flat surfaces of the rocks, and to depict the dark shadows at the left caused by the strong side lighting. The spectators to the left and right of Jesus reveal their astonishment and curiosity at what they see. Clasped hands, staring eyes, and open mouths effectively express their feelings of surprise.[52] Note also the figure of one of the sisters of Lazarus, who is kneeling at the left in a reverent attitude. The intense realism shown in this print is one of the greatest charms of Rembrandt's composition.

The face of Jesus is particularly well done, expressing sorrow ("Jesus wept"),[53] gentleness, and love. He raises his hand in a gentle gesture of compassion.[54] Rembrandt chose to depart somewhat from the Bible text ("The man who had died came out, his hands and feet bound with linen strips, and his face wrapped with a cloth")[55] by picturing Lazarus without the wrappings, perhaps to show the expression of surprise and wonder on his face. Everything in this print is peaceful and serene. Nothing could be added to the plate without impairment, even by the Master himself; it is one of Rembrandt's most perfect compositions.[56]

From time to time Rembrandt turned his attention to etched portraits. In 1641, he produced the magnificent portrait of *Cornelis Claesz.*
Cat. no. 19   *Anslo, Preacher* (B. 271), a cloth merchant who was distantly related to Rembrandt and a Mennonite minister for the Waterland Congregation, a liberal sect in Amsterdam. Anslo wrote theological works in which he defended Mennonite orthodoxy against attacks by Socinians. The Waterland Congregation believed that the Word, whether written or spoken, took precedence over a painted

or drawn image. This belief is illustrated in the print, for Anslo is surrounded by his books but has removed a painting from the wall (the empty nail from which it hung is visible at the upper right) and turned it away from the viewer.[57] This had a symbolic purpose, alluding to the Protestant belief that salvation can only be given through the Word, thus denying the role accorded images by the Catholic Church.[58, 59] A poem commemorating this etching was written by Vondel[60] and is inscribed in a seventeenth-century hand, in Dutch, on an impression of the second state in London: "O Rembrandt, paint Cornelis's voice! His outward appearance is the least of him. What is invisible, one can only learn by ear; he who wants to see Anslo must hear him."[61] In this etching we find a more complete tonality and painterly quality than in any early etched portrait by Rembrandt.

This apparently was a commissioned etching, for a vigorous study in red chalk and white body color, in reverse (Benesch 758), dated 1640, is in the British Museum. That Rembrandt used the chalk study to transfer the drawing to the plate is indicated by, first, the indentations of the sharp point used for transfer, visible on the drawing; second, the back of the drawing is covered with ochre tempera for transfer.[62] In 1640 he did a portrait of Anslo in pen and brown ink with gray and brown washes, corrected with white (Benesch 759; Paris, Musée du Louvre). Rembrandt, in 1641, also painted an oil portrait of Anslo and his wife, Aeltje Gerritsdr. Schouten (Bredius 409; Berlin), in which the preacher's pose is similar to that in the etching. This is a rare, lifetime impression on white, unwashed, and unpressed paper with a deep impression of the plate mark and drypoint burr in several areas of the print.

The year 1642 marks disaster for Rembrandt. Saskia, who in September 1641 bore Titus, their fourth and only child who survived to adulthood, died in June of 1642. The same year witnessed the completion of the great group portrait called *The Night Watch* (Bredius 410; Amsterdam) that Rembrandt painted entirely for the effects of light and shade without giving much consideration to the sitters. Although *The Night Watch* broke certain conventions of sixteenth- and seventeenth-century Dutch group portrait painting, there is little evidence to support the widely accepted myth that his patrons were very dissatisfied with the picture, and that it caused a marked change in his fortune and social life. Available evidence proves that the painting received more praise than criticism.[63] At any rate, from this point on, Rembrandt seems to be a more sincere, humble, and introspective man and yet at the same time much more stubborn and uncompromising, both as an artist and a man, completely disregarding bourgeois conventions.[64]

About 1642 he did the small *Self-Portrait in a Flat Cap and Embroidered Dress* (B. 26), a delicate, masterful sketch. This self-portrait shows Rembrandt in full possession of his skills as an etcher. Early impressions, as this first state, have a very faint signature, *Rembrandt f.*, at the upper left; later the signature was re-engraved by another hand.

Cat. no. 21

Girl with a Basket (B. 356)[65] is done in the same open style as the *Self-Portrait in a Flat Cap and Embroidered Dress* (B. 26) and dates from the same period (ca. 1642). About this etching C. J. Holmes remarked, "Not good…the comparative dullness of the handling merely an example of the frailty of even the greatest executive talents."[66] I disagree. Though the execution is simple and straightforward, the final product is a beautifully drawn and charming genre scene. The drawing in Stockholm, *An Old and a Young Woman in Discussion* (Benesch 738), of about 1642 depicts the girl in reverse and full figure.

Cat. no. 22

This is an excellent, fresh impression of the second state with inky plate edges and light plate tone. The generous margins and the unwashed, unpressed condition of this impression give it a special charm and immediacy.[67] Nowell-Usticke described this print as RRR+ (extremely rare).[68]

About this time, he completed a small plate, *Sheet with Two Studies: A Tree, and the Upper Part of* *Cat. no. 23* *a Head of the Artist Wearing a Velvet Cap* (B. 372). The carefully etched, unfinished self-portrait is reminiscent of a Dutch painting, while the tree is more freely rendered in Rembrandt's mature style. This is a superb, rich impression of an extremely rare print. Incidentally, a similar head with only one eye, the top of the nose and a flat velvet cap appears behind and to the left of the standard bearer in *The Night Watch* (Bredius 410) of 1642.[69]

The following decade of Rembrandt's life was the quietest and most serene as far as external events are concerned. Hendrickje Stoffels joined his household as a maid about 1649 and lived with him through his financial troubles in the 1650s, when he became bankrupt in 1656. During the early 1640s Rembrandt had considered himself a rich man and lived a carefree life as artist and collector with many friends and pupils. Among these, Carel Fabritius, Gerbrand van den Eeckhout, Samuel von Hoogstraten, and Philips de Koninck, to name some of the best known, were then working in his studio.[70]

Rembrandt occasionally pictured animals in his prints. One of the most interesting of these is *Cat. no. 10* *The Small Lion Hunt (with two lions)* (B. 115) of about 1632. This boldly crafted etching demonstrates Rembrandt's great skill with the etching needle. The sense of movement of the two lions is vividly portrayed using a variety of lines. The deeply bitten foreground and horseman at the left frame the subject, whereas the lions and the background figures are lightly etched.[71] Rembrandt may have been inspired here by two engravings by Antonio Tempesta (B. 1132 and 1171), of whose work Rembrandt owned four volumes. The signature and date on the verso, *P. mariette 1661*, indi-

cate this fine impression was in Pierre Mariette's collection during Rembrandt's lifetime.

Another interesting animal study is *The Hog* (B. 157) of 1643, probably intended to illustrate *Cat. no. 24* the slaughtering of a hog. A mother smiles with pleasure at the nervous wonderment of her child stretching forward to touch the hog. Note the small boy behind the sow who holds an inflated pig's bladder. This may hint at a hidden meaning: just like blowing soap bubbles in our day, in the seventeenth century, blowing up a pig's bladder was a familiar symbol of transience.[72] In contrast to the rather sketchily drawn figures in the background, the sow, whose legs are bound ready for slaughter, has been developed in great detail with a combination of etching and vigorous drypoint. The position of the hog is close to that of the reclining hog in the drawing (Benesch 777). This impression is a first state of two according to the catalogue of White-Boon[73] and a second state of three according to the catalogues of G. W. Nowell-Usticke[74] and George Biörklund.[75]

We come now to perhaps what is the most famous and certainly the most popular of all Rembrandt's etchings, known as the "Hundred Guilder Print" (B. 74). The story that Rembrandt bid one *Cat. no. 27* hundred guilders at an auction in order to buy back a single impression of the print appears for the first time in Zacharias Conrad von Uffenbach's diary of his travels of 1711.[76,77] This story was later repeated by Pierre Mariette. A second account of the origin of this title is due to Gersaint, who in his 1751 catalogue (no. 75) states that an impression of this print (*La Pièce de Cent Florins*) was exchanged for several prints by Marcantonio [Raimondi] valued at 100 guilders by an art dealer in Rome. This story probably derives from an inscription on the verso of an impression in the Rijksmuseum that recounts these facts.

This is one of the most important of Rembrandt's etchings, both from its scale and from the ambitious effort involved. It was probably the result of several years' labor and was completed about 1649. Here Christ the Savior stands among the crowd and seeks to help those pressing in upon him. "He stands as a human amongst humans, poor as they are poor and yet still the divine Saviour."[78] It is remarkable how this etching gives the impression that Christ is both near and remote, both divine and human. Rembrandt has been able to impart to Christ's figure a supernatural splendor and at the same time to clothe it with humility. Notice how distinct and earthly is the shadow of the woman's begging hands on the Savior's garment. The etching gives the impression that Christ is one of the people, and yet Rembrandt has made Him taller than the others.[79]

The "Hundred Guilder Print" appears to represent several incidents described in chapter 19 of the Gospel of Matthew. A contemporary poem written by H. F. Waterloo in 1665 on the lower recto of an impression of the second state, now in the Bibliothèque Nationale, Paris, indicates the print's subject is the whole of chapter 19 of Matthew.[80, 81] Thus the right half of the print illustrates verse 2 which describes how "large crowds followed him and he healed them there."

The chapter continues (verses 3–12) with the Pharisees in a discussion with Christ about marriage and the lawfulness of divorce, to which Rembrandt refers indirectly by showing a group of Pharisees arguing among themselves in the left background.

Verses 13 and 14 are illustrated in the left-center of the print: "The children were brought to him that he might lay his hands on them and pray. The disciples rebuked the people, but Jesus said, 'Let the little children come to me and do not hinder them, for to such belongs the kingdom of heaven.'"

Note the child pulling its mother, who carries a baby, toward Christ. Another mother with an infant is already near Christ. Peter, just to the left of Christ, pushes the mother back while looking up to Christ for his approval. Christ's extended right hand invites the mothers and children forward. Sitting on the ground between and to the left of the two mothers is a thoughtful young man who may represent the "rich young man" who decided to keep his riches rather than give them to the poor and follow Christ (verses 16–22). The camel at the extreme right of the print may refer to Christ's words in verses 23–24 after the young man had departed, "And Jesus said to his disciples, 'Truly I say to you, only with difficulty will a rich person enter the kingdom of heaven. Again I tell you, it is easier for a camel to go through the eye of a needle than for a rich person to enter the kingdom of God.'" With this broad interpretation,[82, 83] the print embraces a large part of Rembrandt's view of Christ's work, and in its manifold intent and wonderful insight, it is an epitome of the artist's power of individual expression.[84]

As a composition the "Hundred Guilder Print" relates to his earlier work in its diagonal arrangement of light and shade. Due to his wonderful chiaroscuro, Rembrandt is able to preserve an impressive unity in the composition, in spite of the multitude and variety of its parts.[85] In this single plate we see force, pathos, mystery, complexity, and one of Rembrandt's most effective uses of chiaroscuro. In its boldness of mass and richness of inventive power no other of Rembrandt's prints compares with it.[86]

The manner of the execution, a combination of the fragile burr of drypoint and etching, caused the plate to wear out quickly, and the print must have been intended for only a select few.[87] Ten impressions exist of the first state, all of which are in public collections. After the plate became very worn and corroded it was acquired by an Englishman, Captain Baillie (1723–1810), from the painter and engraver John Greenwood. Baillie skillfully reworked the plate in 1775 and printed one hundred impressions, which he sold for various prices depending on the paper type. Thus a proof on French paper was priced at 2£. 12s. 6d.; one on Indian paper at 4£. 4s.; and one on the finest Japan paper or on satin at 5£. 5s.[88] There are two Baillie retouchings. The first, before the additional drypoint work, is exhibited here. A later, second retouching shows much additional drypoint work on the straw to the left of the woman's foot and on the dog's body. About 1776, the plate was cut into four pieces and impressions taken from each piece.[89]

Cat. no. 28 The book of Tobit[90] in the Apocrypha served as a source for several of Rembrandt's subjects. One of his finest etchings is from this source, *The Blindness of Tobit: The Larger Plate* (B. 42), signed twice: *Rembrandt f. 1651.* Tobit, a God-fearing Jew, exiled to Nineveh where he had an accident that left him blind and beset by numerous troubles, sent his son Tobias to his kinsman, Gabael, at Rages in Media to collect a large sum of money (ten talents of silver) that he had left in trust with him. Tobias was accompanied on his quest by the angel Raphael, disguised as a distant relative, Azariah, who advised him to catch a fish from the Tigris River and save its heart, liver, and gall. They interrupted their journey at the house of a relative of Tobit's, Raguel, in Ecbatana where Tobias married Raguel's daughter, Sarah, and received a substantial dowry as a result. Tobias was able, by burning the fish's heart and liver in their bedroom, to drive off a demon, Asmodeus, who had killed her first seven husbands on their wedding nights. After receiving the money from Gabael in Media, the newlyweds and the angel Raphael returned to Tobias's home. Tobit and his wife Anna knew nothing of these adventures and were alarmed by the long delay. The moment depicted here follows Anna's telling Tobit that Tobias is on the road outside their home. Tobit gropes his way toward the

door to greet his son and, in his haste, he knocks over the spinning wheel; his little dog tries to guide him and leaps about by his feet. Subsequently, Tobias anointed Tobit's eyes with the fish gall and healed his father's blindness.[91]

This is a beautiful impression of the first state of two. The printing is crisp, bright, and particularly effective on the blank wall by the door, where a streak of tone gives texture. The emphatic drypoint work under Tobit's feet heightens the illusion of his stumbling progress to the door.[92] For his figure of the blind Tobit Rembrandt has borrowed the figure of *The Blinding of Elymas* from a 1516 engraving by Agostino Veneziano (B. 43) after a Raphael tapestry cartoon.[93, 94]

In the lower margin is an interesting inscription by Sir Francis Seymour Haden, English surgeon, amateur etcher of distinction, and a great connoisseur and fastidious collector of Rembrandt's etchings: "To Richard Fisher, Esq. – a print of no value – but certainly one of the *best* of Rembrandt's work. S. Haden."

We come now to the period of Rembrandt's greatest maturity. We find an increase in the vigor and breadth of the treatment. The lines of shading are more open, the touch truer and more spontaneous. Drypoint is used more and more frequently.

In 1654 Rembrandt did possibly his only series of a single subject matter, a set of six etchings (B. 45, 47, 55, 60, 63, 64) illustrating scenes from the childhood of Christ. With the exception of B. 45, all are about the same size; they comprise a stylistic and thematic unit that emphasizes humble events in the boyhood of Christ.

One of these, *The Circumcision in the Stable* (B. 47), is a plate illustrating Rembrandt's command of reflected light. He is able to attain an element of mystery in this plate. The line of dark shadow on the right cutting the shepherd's head is a bit forceful. And yet we should remember that without experiments of this kind we should not *Cat. no. 30* possess some of Rembrandt's most daring and splendid conceptions.[95] The Bible does not indicate where the circumcision (performed on the eighth day after birth)[96] took place, but since Mosaic Law forbade the mother to enter the temple until forty days after giving birth to a male child,[97] the Apocryphal books usually locate the circumcision in a stable. Despite this, in Western iconography the scene has been traditionally placed in the Temple, with the high priest performing the ceremony. Rembrandt followed the Western iconographical tradition in his circumcision etchings of Gersaint 48 (ca. 1626) and Bartsch 48 (ca. 1630). The criticism of seventeenth-century commentators probably induced Rembrandt to locate this late work of the circumcision in a stable, instead of the Temple.[98]

This impression is one of the exceedingly rare trial proofs (Hind 274 i)[99] before the plate corners were rounded. It is printed on a soft, absorbent paper that gives a slightly woolly effect to the lines. Rembrandt used this type of paper for study proofs of a few of his etchings of 1654.

This print's provenance is very interesting. Dr. Karel G. Boon, former director of the Rijksmuseum's collection of prints and drawings in Amsterdam, indicated he believed that the print came from the Willem Six collection that derived from Rembrandt's own personal collection.[100] This collection was sold to Jacob Houbraken in 1734. It then passed to Peter Cornelis Baron van Leyden in 1739, to Johan Gail in 1788, and then to Mme. Gail. It was purchased by the Rijksmuseum in 1808 and later sold in 1882 by the then director as a supposed duplicate. The stamp (Lugt 240) of the Royal Library on the verso is the earliest associated with the Rijksmuseum and was introduced in 1808 under Louis Bonaparte, King of Holland (1806–1820). It is found in particular on prints that formed the important van Leyden collection, purchased by the Rijksmuseum in 1808.

A wonderful print of an Old Testament subject is *Abraham's Sacrifice* (B. 35) of 1655. To test Abraham, God asked that he offer his son Isaac as a sacrifice. When they arrived at the place God had appointed, Isaac asked, "My Father.... Behold the fire and the wood, but where is the lamb for a burnt offering?" Abraham replied, "God will provide for himself the lamb for a burnt offering, my son."[101] The print depicts the moment when Abraham is about to slay his son. An angel stops Abraham, saying, "Do not lay your hand on the boy or do anything to him, for now I know that you fear God, seeing you have not withheld your son, your only son, from me."[102] Rembrandt has followed the iconographical tradition and depicted the angel grasping Abraham's arm, rather than following the Bible text. The main figure is defined in the strict and simple forms of Rembrandt's style of the 1650s. The three figures of the central group are merged into a compact form nearly resembling a sculpture in the round. The bright, peaceful view into the distant background and the waiting servants with their donkey form a strong contrast with the main figures, illuminated in the midst of darkness by a powerful shaft of light.[103]

Cat. no. 31

This is a fine impression with drypoint burr below the angel's right elbow, on the dark spot just below Abraham's beard and on the vertical lines below and to the left of the large basin at the lower center of the print.

Christ Appearing to the Apostles (B. 89), signed and dated *Rembrandt f. 1656*, is a magnificent print in a loose, sketchy technique and open form. It is one of Rembrandt's most lightly sketched plates. Christopher White captures well the spirit of this print:

Cat. no. 32

> Here he is portraying the miraculous and mystical light that radiates from the tall, wraith-like figure of Christ dissolving all human matter. Christ is a glowing figure whose brightness is painful to behold for human onlookers. We sense

his sudden appearance through locked doors. Nothing mortal could contain him…. He obtains …radiance in the print by the use of long parallel lines of shading, muting the bodily reality of each figure, which recall the technique of the engraver. The freedom and effortlessness of the final appearance of the plate belie the struggle that went into this work.[104]

According to the account in chapter 20 of the Gospel of John, Christ appeared to his disciples the evening of the resurrection and displayed the wounds in his hands, feet, and side. Thomas was absent and, when informed later by the other disciples, "We have seen the Lord," he declared, "Unless I see in his hands the mark of the nails, and place my finger into the mark of the nails, and place my hand into his side, I will never believe."[105] When Christ made his second appearance to his disciples eight days later, Thomas was present. Jesus said to Thomas, "Put your finger here, and see my hands, and put out your hand, and place it in my side. Do not disbelieve, but believe." Thomas answered him, "My Lord and my God."[106]

Christopher White identifies this etching with the first appearance of Christ and the kneeling figure as Peter.[107] Others, such as J. P. Filedt Kok,[108] believe the etching represents Christ's second appearing and the kneeling figure as Thomas. I think the print represents Christ's second appearance since he seems to be drawing the attention of the kneeling figure to the wound in his side. Also, the account in John makes no specific mention of Peter, but does focus on Thomas's initial skepticism and later belief in Christ's resurrection. Interestingly, this print was described in the catalogue of Valerius Röver's collection and afterwards by Bartsch as "Christ Giving the Keys to St. Peter." In subsequent Rembrandt catalogues up to and including that of Hind, the print was interpreted as "The Incredulity of Thomas." The correct title was pointed out by Werner Weisbach.[109] Nowell-Usticke describes the rarity of this print as RRRR – "a great rarity."[110]

Münz suggests that from this time forward, Rembrandt is driven by a strange impulse to seize and fix in etching the most personal and evanescent impressions against all the rules of graphic art. This results in a multiplicity of states of each plate, states that are no longer so much working proofs as expressions of Rembrandt's capricious moods. It also brought about a change of technique, a technique which combines etching, drypoint, and engraving in each plate. In these years Rembrandt continued exploring and discovering.[111] As far as we know, there are no Rembrandt etchings after 1665, though he continued to paint until his death on October 4, 1669.

In respect to art, granting a supreme design, the criterion of greatness is the spiritual element or the humanity that permeates the work. A careful study of Rembrandt's etchings should convince one that "no one has expressed the human spirit through his art more completely than Rembrandt, and that to find equal manifestations of such expressive power, one would need to seek it in masters of other arts; for example, Shakespeare in poetry and prose, or Beethoven in music."[112]

S. William Pelletier
*Emeritus Alumni Foundation Distinguished Professor of Chemistry
Emeritus Director of the Institute for Natural Products Research
The University of Georgia*

ENDNOTES

1 Arthur M. Hind, *A History of Engraving and Etching from the 15th Century to the Year 1914*. London: Houghton Mifflin Co., 1923, p. 170. New York: Dover Publications, Inc. 1963.

2 Richard Godfrey, "Introduction" in Nancy Bialler, Adrian T. Eeles, Richard Godfrey and Katharina Mayer Haunton, *A Collection of Etchings by Rembrandt Harmensz. van Rijn (1606–1669) formed by Joseph R. Ritman*: presented for sale by Artemis and Sotheby's. Amsterdam: Mees Pierson, [1995]. (Hereafter referred to as the *Ritman Catalogue*.)

3 J. Orlers, *Beschrijvinge der Stadt Leiden*, second edition. Leiden, 1641, p. 375. Transcribed in Seymour Slive, *Rembrandt and His Critics, 1630–1730*. The Hague: Martinus Nijhoff, 1953, p. 203.

4 Christopher White, *Rembrandt and His World*. London: Thames and Hudson, 1964, p. 5.

5 A. Bredius, *Rembrandt. The Complete Edition of the Paintings*, third edition. (Revised by H. Gerson.) London and New York: Phaidon, 1969.

6 Etching goes back to the early years of the sixteenth century. It involves the process of drawing with a needle through a protective acid-resistant varnish called a ground, laid down on the surface of a polished copper, zinc or other metal plate. The artist's lines are etched through the ground to expose the metallic surface beneath. After completion of the drawing the plate is immersed in an acid bath (usually nitric acid or Dutch mordant). The lines are etched or bitten by the acid wherever the metal is exposed, while areas of the plate protected by the ground remain untouched.

The depth of the etched line depends on the length of time the plate remains in the acid bath. Lines that have been bitten deeply enough can be protected from further action of the acid by application of an acid-resistant varnish, a process called "stopping out." When suitably etched, the ground is removed and the plate is covered with a thick ink, the ink being rubbed well into the lines. After the excess ink is removed, the plate is printed by passing it, covered with a sheet of damp paper, through a press under heavy pressure. As the damp paper is forced into the lines on the plate, the ink is transferred to the paper. The resulting impression of the design originally etched on the plate (in reverse) is called an etching. The genius of etching lies in its lively, flexible, and expressive line. It has almost all the freedom of an original drawing (since the ground offers little resistance to the needle) and therefore is capable of infinite variation. The only difference from a drawing is in the character of the etched line itself, and it is this character that is the chief charm and delight of an etching. In general, early states of Rembrandt etchings are most desirable. In these the etched lines are clear and strong, and where drypoint occurs, the burr is rich and full-bodied. In later states the etched lines are weaker and in drypoint lines, the burr is weak or nonexistent.

7 Hind, *A History*, p. 172.

8 Drypoint involves drawing with a needle or diamond point on bare metal, throwing up a ragged metal curl (burr) on each side of the incised line. Not only the line, but the metal curl holds printing ink, with the result that when the plate is printed the impression shows a furry, velvety texture (burr) along the lines. Since the burr is raised above the plate surface, it wears away very quickly under pressure.

9 Hind, *A History*, p. 172.

10 Edmé-François Gersaint, *Catalogue raisonné de toutes les pièces qui forment l'oeuvre de Rembrandt*. Paris, 1751.

11 Woldemar von Seidlitz, *Kritisches Verzeichniss der Radierungen Rembrandts*. Leipzig, 1922.

12 Christopher White and Karel G. Boon, *Hollstein's Dutch and Flemish Etchings, Engravings and Woodcuts*, volumes XVIII and XIX, *Rembrandt van Rijn*. Amsterdam: A. L. van Gendt & Co., 1969.

13 See, for example, Ludwig Münz, *Rembrandt's Etchings*, vol. 1. London: Phaidon Press, 1952, pp. 1–2.

14 *Ibid.*, p. 2.

15 *Ibid.*

16 Adam Bartsch, *Catalogue Raisonné de toutes les Estampes qui forment l'Oeuvre de Rembrandt, et ceux de ses principaux Imitateurs*. Vienna, 1797, 2 volumes. Hereafter abbreviated as B.

17 K. G. Boon, *Rembrandt: the complete Etchings*. London: Thames and Hudson, 1963, p. 17.

18 *Ritman Catalogue*, no. 119.

19 C. J. Holmes, *Notes on the Art of Rembrandt*. London: Chatto & Windus, 1911, p. 205.

20 The term "state" refers to variation within the printed edition. During the process of preparing a plate the artist may print one or more impressions to judge the quality of the work thus far. These impressions are in the "first state." On examining these impressions the artist may decide to make additions or corrections on the plate. Impressions printed after these changes would then constitute a "second state," etc.

21 Münz, vol.1, p. 19.

22 *Ritman Catalogue*, no. 69.

23 J. P. Filedt Kok, *Rembrandt etchings and drawings in the Rembrandt House. A Catalogue*. Maarssen: Gary Schwartz, 1972, p. 109.

24 Jules Lieure, *Jacques Callot: La vie artistique et catalogue raisonné*. Second edition revised, 5 vols. Paris, Editions de la Gazette des Beaux-Arts, 1924–1929. Third edition revised, 8 vols. New York: Collectors Editions Ltd., 1969.

25 Richard Godfrey in "Introduction," *Ritman Catalogue*.

26 Hilliard T. Goldfarb, *A Humanist Vision. The Adolph Weil, Jr. Collection of Rembrandt Prints*. Hanover, New Hampshire: Hood Museum of Art, Dartmouth College, 1988, p. 76, no. 28.

27 Luke 2:22–38. Scripture references are from *The Holy Bible. English Standard Version*. Wheaton, IL: Crossway Bibles, 2001.

28 Filedt Kok, p. 55, B. 51.

29 *Ritman Catalogue*, no. 29.

30 *Ibid.*

31 Genesis 37:31–34.

32 Matthew 22:15–21.

33 *Ritman Catalogue*, no. 57.

34 Münz, vol.1, p. 24.

35 F. Schmidt-Degener, *Catalogus van de Verzameling Etsen van Rembrandt in het bezit van I. de Bruijn*. The Hague, 1932, p. 230.

36 Dieuwke de Hoop Scheffer, "Petrus Sylvius par Rembrandt," in *Liber Amicorum Karel G. Boon*. Amsterdam: Swets & Zeitlinger BV, 1974, pp. 96–101.

37 *Ritman Catalogue*, no. 102. In most recent catalogues of Rembrandt's etchings this impression matches the description for state two

of two. The unique impression of the so-called first state in Paris is regarded by G. W. Nowell-Usticke and Adrian Eeles as a falsification. Thus, there appears to be a single state of this etching.

38 Emile Michel, *Rembrandt, His Life, His Work and His Time*. London: William Heinemann, 1903, p. 183.

39 Loys Delteil, *Le Peintre-Graveur Illustré: Edgar Degas*. Vol. 9. Paris: Chez l'Auteur, 1919, no. 5. Reprint, *Le Peintre-Graveur Illustré: Degas*. Vol. IX. New York: Collectors Editions Ltd. Da Capo Press, 1969, no. 5.

40 Arthur M. Hind, *Rembrandt*. The Charles Eliot Norton Lectures. London: Humphrey Milford; Oxford University Press, 1938, p. 80.

41 Richard Godfrey in "Introduction," *Ritman Catalogue*.

42 Genesis 37:2–10.

43 Holmes, p. 231, no. 160.

44 Arnold Houbraken, *De Groote Schouburgh der Nederlantsche Konstschilders en Schilderessen*, vol. 1. Amsterdam, 1718. Translated in T. Borenius, *Rembrandt. Selected Paintings*. London: Phaidon Press, 1944, p. 27.

45 Münz, vol.1, p. 28.

46 Cynthia P. Schneider, *Rembrandt's Landscapes. Drawings and Prints*. Washington, D. C.: National Gallery of Art, 1990, pp. 37–38, 85 (no. 7).

47 Otto Benesch, *The Drawings of Rembrandt*. 6 vols. London: Phaidon Press Ltd., 1954–1957. Enlarged edition, London: Phaidon Press Ltd., 1973.

48 Holmes, p. 239, no. 206.

49 John 11:39.

50 John 11:40.

51 John 11:43.

52 Christopher White, *Rembrandt as an Etcher. A Study of the Artist at Work*, second edition. New Haven and London: Yale University Press, 1999, pp. 48–49.

53 John 11:35.

54 Hans-Martin Rotermund. *Rembrandt's Drawings and Etchings of the Bible*. Philadelphia: United Church Press, 1969, p. 188.

55 John 11:44.

56 Hind, *A History*, p. 177.

57 *Ritman Catalogue*, no. 106.

58 White, *Rembrandt as an Etcher*, p. 138.

59 W. Busch, "Zu Rembrandts Anslo-Radierung," *Oud Holland*, 1971, 86, pp. 196–199.

60 W. Strauss and M. van der Meulen (with S. Dudok van Heel and P. de Baar), *The Rembrandt Documents*. New York, 1979, no. 1644/6.

61 White, *Rembrandt as an Etcher*, p. 138.

62 P. Morse, "Rembrandt's Etching Technique: An Example" in *U.S. National Museum Bulletin*, 1966, no. 250, p. 100 and footnote 25.

63 Seymour Slive, *Rembrandt and His Critics, 1630–1730*. The Hague: Martinus Nijhoff, 1953, pp. 4–6, 108.

64 Münz, vol. 1, p. 28.

65 Paul Prouté S. A., Paris, catalogue *Géricault*, 1990, no. 146, to Pace Prints, New York, June 1990 to Artemis Fine Arts Ltd., London, to Joseph R. Ritman, Amsterdam, 1990.

66 Holmes, p. 237, no. 195.

67 *Ritman Catalogue*, no. 120.

68 G. W. Nowell-Usticke, *Rembrandt's Etchings, States and Values*. Narberth, PA: Livingston Publishing Co., 1967, no. 356.

69 George Biörklund, with the assistance of Osbert H. Barnard, *Rembrandt's Etchings True and False. A Summary Catalogue*, second edition. Stockholm, London, New York, 1968, p. 92, no. BB 42–1.

70 Münz, vol. 1, pp. 28–29.

71 *Ritman Catalogue*, no. 65.

72 Eva Ornstein-Van Slooten, Marijke Holtrop, and Peter Schatborn, *The Rembrandt House: a catalogue of Rembrandt's etchings*. Amsterdam: Museum het Rembrandthuis, n.d., p. 87, no. 157.

73 White and Boon, no. 157.

74 Nowell-Usticke, *Rembrandt's Etchings*, no. 157.

75 Biörklund, *Rembrandt's Etchings True and False*, p. 94, no. 43-A.

76 Zacharias Conrad von Uffenbach, *Merkwürdige Reisen durch Niedersachsen Holland und Engelland*. Ulm. 1753, III, p. 581.

77 Slive, p. 167.

78 Münz, vol. 1, p. 37.

79 *Ibid.*, pp. 37–38.

80 Filedt Kok, p. 66.

81 White, *Rembrandt as an Etcher*, p. 54.

82 *Ibid.*

83 Münz, vol. 2, p. 102.

84 Hind, *Rembrandt*, pp. 65–66.

85 *Ibid.*, p. 66.

86 Holmes, pp. 97-98.

87 Münz, vol. 1, p. 38.

88 *140 Radierungen von Rembrandt der Jahre 1629 bis 1665*. Bern: Ausstellung Galerie Kornfeld, Bern, March 19 – April 28, 1979, no. 45.

89 Nowell-Usticke, *Rembrandt's Etchings*, no. 74.

90 *Tobit* in *The New Oxford Annotated Bible. New Revised Standard Version*. Edited by Bruce M. Metzger and Roland E. Murphy. New York: Oxford University Press, 1991, *Apocrypha*, pp. 2–19.

91 *Tobit*, pp. 2–19.

92 *Ritman Catalogue*, no. 19.

93 White, *Rembrandt as an Etcher*, pp. 265–266, note 4.

94 Münz, vol. 2, no. 181.

95 Holmes, p. 252, no. 274.

96 Luke 2:21.

97 Leviticus 12:1–4.

98 Filedt Kok, p. 53, no. 47.

99 Arthur M. Hind, *A Catalogue of Rembrandt's Etchings*, second edition. London: Methuen and Co. Ltd., 1923, no. 274, st.i. Reprint: New York: Da Capo Press, 1967.

100 Conversation with the author in the Rijksprentenkabinet of the Rijksmuseum on July 23, 1968.

101 Genesis 22:8.

102 Genesis 22:12.

103 Filedt Kok, pp. 42–43.

104 Christopher White, *Rembrandt as an Etcher. A study of the artist at work*. London: A. Zwemmer Ltd., 1969, p. 95.

105 John 20:25.

106 John 20:27–28.

107 White, *Rembrandt as an Etcher*, 1999, pp. 107–108.

108 Filedt Kok, pp. 81–82.

109 Werner Weisbach, *Rembrandt*. Berlin and Leipzig: Verlag Walter de Gruyter & Co., 1926, p. 437.

110 Nowell-Usticke, *Rembrandt's Etchings*, no. 89.

111 Münz, vol. 1, pp. 55–56.

112 Hind, *Rembrandt*, pp. 134–135.

Christ Appearing to the Apostles
(cat. no. 32), detail, enlarged

Why Study Prints?*

"The art scholars who read all day long are like people who study cookbooks to satisfy their hunger."

—MAX FRIEDLÄNDER

My close encounters with old master prints began at the Fogg Museum at Harvard University, whose print room during my graduate student years was under the care of a benevolent dragon named Ruth Magurn. A quiet, gray-haired curator, trained by the great Jakob Rosenberg, Miss Magurn never hoarded her precious paper materials as do many who are obsessed by the fragility of the objects in their care. Still, she too kept a sharp eye on visitors, and decades later I well remember the force of her relentless gaze on the back of my neck. After months of creeping cautiously into the print room to explore the vast Dutch holdings at the Fogg (at times in the company of Cornell's Frank

Robinson), I arrived on a day that seemed at first like any other. At long last, however, Miss Magurn rose to her feet, strolled into her inner office and remained there, leaving me alone with the Rembrandts. Such coming-of-age experiences are rare in anyone's lifetime.

Having original works of art available for examination is not, ever, to be treated lightly or taken for granted, least of all by students of art or art history in colleges and universities. The objects of our study call for the closest visual scrutiny, yet day after day most of us lecture and listen in darkened rooms to slides or Power Point projections that are all shameless liars. A college or university collection, or the presence of borrowed works, transforms our enterprise, and it is worth remembering how long the museum's importance to the academy has been recognized in this country.

Early American educators were well aware of art's capacity to civilize and broaden youthful minds – not only through developing the taste and esthetic discrimination that were believed to elevate spiritual and ethical standards, but also to encourage deeper understanding of the past and greater tolerance toward foreign cultures. Thomas Jefferson's original goals for the University of Vir-

*NOTE: Portions of these remarks have been adapted from two more extensive articles by this author to which the reader is referred for further material and references on the role of original works of art in the development of American educational institutions and on the importance of old master prints in the instruction of undergraduates:

"Dutch Art in Academia: Observations on College and University Collecting,"

pp. 79–103 in *Hollandse Meesters uit Amerika; Great Dutch Paintings from America*, Royal Picture Gallery, Mauritshuis, The Hague; The Fine Arts Museums of San Francisco, September 1990 – May 1991.

"Dürer and Rembrandt in Academia," pp. 23–45 in *The Felix M. Warburg Print Collection. A Legacy of Discernment*, Frances Lehman Loeb Art Center, Vassar College, Poughkeepsie, New York, 1995.

ginia included the fine arts as an integral part of the curriculum. Since the late eighteenth century, college and university art collections have proliferated so widely that they now comprise roughly one-third of all the art museums in the United States. It is astonishing to realize that they actually predate, by more than a generation, the major public museums that only began to be founded in American cities during the 1870s.

The impetus for making original works available for study relates closely to the distinctively residential character of American colleges and universities, many of which were established in beautiful but remote surroundings. Because students live on these campuses during some of the liveliest and most formative years of their lives, they often come to feel a deep and lasting connection to the place, its setting and its resources. Works of art studied in a context that encourages prolonged and repeated contemplation tend to be treasured in a highly personal, even proprietary way. Indeed, a painting or etching that has been the topic of a term paper or a seminar report becomes the writer's permanent possession, remembered even more vividly than the course itself. It is therefore not surprising that alumni and alumnae have shown such sustained interest in the development of their alma maters' collections. If people give to public museums to be remembered by the world at large or to benefit society, they often give to their colleges and universities, one might say, for the good of the family. The acquisition and study of prints have played an important role in this story.

All prints are, by definition, reproducible, since the printmaking process involves the creation of a master image on a plate (or block or stone) that is then printed in multiple impressions, normally on paper. Distinctions must be made, however, between prints as original conceptions intended for study in their own right, prints as copies, and printed reproductions, which may record works of art made in entirely different media. Each of these categories of printed image has served important purposes for scholars and students and, in fact, all continue to do so.

In the late nineteenth century, when the teaching of art began to find a place in the American college curriculum, new kinds of reproductive prints (wood or electrotype engravings and lithographs along with plaster casts) served as the principal, sometimes the only, models for instruction, along with photographs of foreign sites. If the purpose of such images was to make available to students great works from distant times and places, their manufacturers sometimes took great liberties with the materials at hand, abbreviating or revising the original objects with the intention of clarifying their appearance or meaning. Through a kind of reproductive synecdoche, such early study aids might recall an original in its entirety by concentration on its most salient part – Athena's helmet, Dürer's intricately twisted locks of hair, or Rembrandt's beret.

The easy availability of commercially printed reproductions during this period coincided with and may even have helped foster a developing appreciation for original prints. Interestingly, the extensive collection of America's first great print connoisseur, Francis Calley Gray (who had begun by honing his visual skills on the classification of shells), consisted of fine engraved reproductions after famous paintings as well as important original prints by artists such as Dürer and Rembrandt. In 1857, four thousand of Gray's prints were given to Harvard University, which has continued to add, by purchase and gift, the materials that constitute the Fogg's remarkable print collection today. Building a print collection has always made sense for educational institutions whose acquisition funds tend to be limited. As Professor Charles Eliot

Norton of Harvard observed in 1897:

> "[Prints] are not of less importance as a means of culture and as a means of civilization, than original works of painting and sculpture....They are the only original works of great artists of which the University can hope to possess any considerable collection."

But the educational value of prints had already been recognized much earlier. Beginning with the invention of printmaking itself in the mid-fifteenth century, artists have made and collected original prints not only to inform themselves about the work of other artists, but also as a means of teaching their students about drawing, which has always been considered the most fundamental exercise in artistic training. Rembrandt's emphasis on teaching graphic technique has been well documented by the numbers of his students' sketches that display obvious borrowings from his own drawings or prints, some of these sheets bearing actual corrections by the master himself. A passionate print collector himself, Rembrandt once bid 1,400 guilders at auction for fourteen engravings by Lucas van Leyden – almost the amount of his fee for painting *The Night Watch*. The extent of his collecting activities becomes clear when one examines his 1656 bankruptcy inventory, which lists more than thirty albums of prints by northern and Italian artists, among them a complete set of his own etchings. For many artists, including both Rembrandt and Rubens, the production of prints was also valued as a means of spreading a master's reputation to a larger audience, or even of copyrighting the designs of important paintings.

The collecting and educational use of original prints as repositories of information has been no less historically important, for as early as the mid-sixteenth century large collections of printed images began to be assembled with the purpose of gathering and classifying knowledge according to subject. Encyclopedic museums on paper, seeking to encapsulate universal knowledge, increased during the seventeenth century, a period of growing print production and diversification of subject matter. Such collections characteristically included representations of religious and mythological themes, allegories, historical events, landscapes, specimens of flora and fauna, geographical and scientific materials, and most of all likenesses of famous people representing the various ages of history. Yet appreciation of artistic virtuosity, regardless of subject, was also evident in early print collections. Even in his own lifetime, serious collectors of Rembrandt's prints enthusiastically sought to acquire all the states or stages of completion of his etchings – an indication that his working process was as deeply interesting to them as his choice of subjects.

The eighteenth century saw the formation of even more extensive print collections, as a burgeoning art market (particularly avid for Rembrandt's prints and paintings) encouraged publication of the first comprehensive print catalogues that encouraged comparison of various states of the same prints. The first printed catalogue raisonné of Rembrandt's prints, by the well-known art dealer Edmé-François Gersaint, appeared in 1751, forming the basis of Adam Bartsch's catalogue of 1797. Shortly thereafter Bartsch began the monumental publication of his vast and encyclopedic *Le Peintre-graveur* whose twenty-one volumes appeared between 1803 and 1821. To this day, master prints are handily classified by the distinctive capital "B" abbreviation, followed by their Bartsch numbers.

Prints no longer bear the responsibility of being the primary repositories of visual information, for which we now have other devices that hold more data and organize and retrieve it far more rapidly. Nonetheless, their capacity to inform and delight remains undiminished, even enhanced, because of the close and careful scrutiny they require. This unhurried attention is often a very new experience for students who find that the admonition to stop and proceed very slowly can yield unexpected pleasures. For an instructor there are few classroom experiences more rewarding than observing students encounter an original Rembrandt etching for the first time. Taken aback by the tiny size of images they had come to know only as vast blow-ups on a classroom wall, they are soon closely involved with eyes and magnifying glasses, stunned and delighted at how much more they can see and at how much more intricate and alive the work becomes in person. As every student of Rembrandt discovers, one does not "solve" his images as if they were problems or puzzles; one rather works through them slowly and patiently, hoping only to see them more clearly. Indeed, anyone who spends time with prints comes to realize that the subject represented can only be fully understood through awareness of the eloquence and energy of line itself – individually inscribed, but also hatched or webbed or stippled into areas of tone.

To examine line, which records an artist's touch, is to become aware that the image is the product of multiple decisions and gestures and that the act of seeing it can be a means of partially reconstituting the process through which it was made. Prints, like drawings, disclose through their accumulation of graphic marks the artist's performance of an idea. While the image in its totality exists perpetually in the present, lines chronicle the temporal process that brought it into being. Looking at prints allows one to partake in that process. Through the artist's manipulation of line, forms and textures materialize on the page; where line is absent the page is not vacant, for space or light or surface or sky may be implied, but always through reference to adjacent or surrounding lines. The surface of a print by Rembrandt remains visu-

ally eventful everywhere, as lines shift direction or size or density, changing from orderly parallel hatchings to twists or hooks or short dashes of ink. Areas occupied and unoccupied by line coexist in an intriguingly vibrant state of tension, for each depends upon light-dark contrast with its opposite in order to be perceived and interpreted by the observer.

Rembrandt made use of all the intaglio processes (engraving, etching, and drypoint) which involve the production of lines that are recessed or indented into a metal (usually copper) plate, which is warmed, then inked and wiped so that the ink remains in the etched or engraved depressions. When the plate is forced under pressure through a printing press, the lines are absorbed by the dampened paper and they print as very slightly raised. Thus, even more than drawings, prints are fundamentally process-productions, because the mechanical act of printing intervenes between the initial stage of drawing on the plate and seeing the drawing presented on paper. In all cases, the final product looks significantly different from what the artist drew, because printing reverses the image, replacing pale, indented grooves in a metal plate with inked raised lines on paper. Etching, the most complex of the intaglio processes, adds yet another stage of chemical intervention, in which drawing on a resin-coated plate exposes underlying copper lines that are bitten in an acid bath before printing. To put it plainly, the process is a lot of trouble, hard to handle, and the results can be alarmingly unpredictable. Yet Rembrandt was clearly stimulated by the very aspects of the medium that have turned so many others away from it. That it engages the artist in stages of work that call for constant rethinking and revision clearly interested him deeply.

The exhibition of Rembrandt's prints currently on view at Cornell University illustrates the extraordinary span and diversity of Rembrandt's prints in style as well as subject matter, for it encompasses examples from all periods of his career. These include elaborately finished works such as the famous *Christ Preaching* (the so-called "Hundred Guilder Print"), and other major narrative scenes along with portraits, landscapes, and genre pieces. Some exhibit a startling informality of organization and execution that tells us much about Rembrandt's deep creative identification with printmaking.

Cat. no. 27

One curious little sheet of studies, dating from around 1642 (B. 372), shows only the upper part of the artist's head with one eye (a second eye is lightly sketched in vertically above the head) and the soft velvet beret that appears so often in Rembrandt's self-portraits (B. 26) as an attribute of the learned painter because of its double associations with academic regalia and Renaissance artists' working attire. Above the beret is a tree with a figure standing beside it and seen horizontally when one views the artist's face, so that the shape of the tree roughly parallels the broad shape of the beret. Strands of hair sketched at the right beneath the foliage recall an observation made by the Dutch art theorist Karel van Mander, writing in 1604, who said that leaves, like air, hair and fabrics, require exercise of the artist's imagination (*geest*). In Rembrandt's print the juxtaposition of the artist's penetrating gaze with the motifs of beret and tree make this apparently random series of sketches into a strikingly coherent statement about the relationship between direct examination of nature and artistic imagination in the formation of pictorial imagery. From van Mander on, the Dutch articulated this distinction in two phrases: *naer het leven* ("taken from life") and *uit den geest* ("taken from the imagination").

Cat. no. 23

Cat. no. 21

A few years later, in 1645, Rembrandt made *Cottages and Farm Buildings with a Man Sketching* (B. 219), a freely and confidently sketched view of his local countryside that shows a typical thatched-

Cat. no. 25

roof farmhouse whose distinctive shape is silhouetted against the sky. Variations in the direction of hatched lines model the interesting shapes of this building beyond which, very lightly etched, are the low, flat fields of the countryside around Amsterdam. Only secondarily do we discover the tiny figure tucked into the right foreground: an artist who sketches the scene from life as a kind of witness figure whose presence certifies that the site has been studied directly from life.

Even as we recognize the scene as a landscape, we experience it equally as a *drawing* of a landscape whose lively, selectively disposed lines re-create the view through an accumulation of vividly defined marks whose arrangement reconstitutes what the artist saw and did, allowing us to see what he saw and to follow the process through which he re-created it on the page. Against the pale paper of the page, rapid hatchings conjure up weathered boards or worn thatch; out of a few rapid hooks and curves a goat and two big barn cats take shape; a series of tiny scribbles becomes a flock of birds in flight. The lines seem charged with energy and one examines them with a sense of growing wonder, for the little draftsman – surely Rembrandt's surrogate – seems in the process of rendering the very scene before us. Since it is possible to see the image both as calligraphy and as representation, one has an uncanny sense, as in so many Rembrandt prints, of looking over the artist's shoulder to directly observe the process that brings it forth.

The opportunity to be brought so close to the creative process is probably the most compelling reason why the study of prints still matters today. Prints make us consider the most fundamental questions that can be asked about art: How can ideas and emotions be given tangible form? What constitutes originality? How do tools and materials shape artistic statements? How is visual knowledge disseminated and absorbed? In encouraging us to become patient observers, prints fos-ter an open-minded projection and identification through which the full complexity and intensity of experience (the artist's and our own) can be rec-ognized and absorbed. Students – and we are all students – need every opportunity to remain flex-ible and open to new experience. Only this makes possible the ongoing evolution through which people continue growing through all phases of life into their best and most interesting selves.

SUSAN DONAHUE KURETSKY
Sara Gibson Blanding Professor of Art
Vassar College

S. William Pelletier (s.w.p.)

Franklin W. Robinson (f.w.r.)

Andrew C. Weislogel (a.c.w.)

Catalogue edited by Andrew C. Weislogel

Note: unless otherwise indicated, all works are reproduced at actual size.

1 *The circumcision*

About 1626
Etching on ivory laid paper.
Bartsch 398; Gersaint 48; Seidlitz 398 ii/ii; White-Boon S. 398 ii/ii.

PLATEMARK:
214–213 × 166–161 mm.

SHEET:
215–214 × 169–166 mm.

INSCRIPTIONS ON PLATE:
Rembrant [sic] *fecit* (not by
the artist), at lower left; *I. P.
Berendrech ex.*, at lower right.

PROVENANCE:
P. Mariette II, Paris (inscr:
P. mariette 1704, on verso;
L. 1799); A. Artaria, Vienna
(L. 33, on verso); Herman
Weber, Bonn (L. 1383, on
verso); Joseph Kuderna,
Vienna (L. 1626a, on verso);
Kennedy Galleries, New
York, October 1, 1966.

S.W.P.

One of Rembrandt's very first attempts at print-making, the *Circumcision* is a somewhat awkward work. In it, we see Rembrandt, aged twenty, laboring with a fistful of hatching and shading techniques which overlap and cancel each other. As in Rembrandt's other early learning piece *The Rest on the Flight into Egypt* of about 1626 (B. 59), which also shows this disorienting zigzag hatching style, the gestures of the figures are too energetic, their facial expressions by turns overstated or wooden. The *Circumcision* also not surprisingly shows some strong borrowings from other prints on this subject, such as Jan Sadeler 1's engraving after Maarten de Vos[1], 1581, and especially Hendrick Goltzius's 1594 *Circumcision* from his engraved series of the *Life of the Virgin*. From the Goltzius print, in addition to the general grouping of the figures, Rembrandt takes the anecdotal details of the candle-holder on the wall and the silver plate on the floor. Rembrandt also borrows the pince-nez spectacles from the priest wielding the knife in Goltzius's print, giving them instead to an onlooker in his etching who peers comically through them down at the action. But despite the awkwardness of much of this print, Rembrandt's ability to understand biblical situations in purely human terms still comes out. Joseph (with perhaps Mary beside him), instead of standing stoically by as in Goltzius's engraving, expresses a perfectly understandable measure of parental anxiety about the pain being inflicted on his child.

A.C.W.

---

1 Ludwig Münz, *Rembrandt's Etchings*, vol. 1.
London: Phaidon Press, 1952, p. 1.

Rembrant f.   I. P. Berendrecht. ex.

I

2 *The artist's mother, head and bust: three quarters right*

1628
Etching and drypoint.
Bartsch 354; Biörklund-Barnard 28A i-ii/ii; Hind 1 i-ii/ii; Münz 82 i-ii/ii;
Nowell-Usticke 354 i-ii/ii; Ritman 119 i-ii/ii; Seidlitz 354 i-ii/ii; White-Boon 354 i-ii/ii.

PLATEMARK:
67.0–66.0 × 63.0–63.5 mm.

SHEET:
68.5–67.5 × 65.0–64.5 mm.

INSCRIPTION ON PLATE:
R–L 1628 (the 2 reversed),
at upper right.

INSCRIPTIONS AND
MARKS ON SHEET:
On verso: *OO* [graphite];
Sotheby's, London/May 16,
1980, lot 109; *Joseph R.
Ritman/cat. no. 119 (1995)*
[graphite]; stamp of S. W.
Pelletier [reddish-brown
ink] (1998; 12.11.35);
Sotheby's, London, May 16,
1980, lot 109 [graphite];
Du H (?).

PROVENANCE:
French collection; [Sotheby
Parke Bernet, London, 1980,
lot 109]; Joseph R. Ritman,
Amsterdam (not in Lugt),
cat. 1995, no. 119; Artemis
SA – Luxembourg Succur-
sale de Genève, purchased
on invoice #99/0019,
December 11, 1998.

DESCRIPTION:
An excellent, early impression in black ink on ivory,
laid paper, printed with
light plate tone, and inky
plate edges. This is a previously unrecorded interme-
diate state between the first
and second, i. e., the face
and bust are completed as
in the usual second state,
but before the plate dimen-
sions were reduced to
65 × 63 mm. Nowell-
Usticke described this print
as R (rare).

LITERATURE:
*Important Old Master
Engravings, Etchings and
Woodcuts*. London: Sotheby
Parke Bernet & Co., May
16, 1980, lot 109 (illustrated
on p. 78); *A Collection of
Etchings by Rembrandt
Harmensz. van Rijn (1606–
1669) formed by Joseph R.
Ritman*. London: Artemis
and Sotheby's [1995],
no. 119 (illustrated).

EXHIBITED:
Mees Pierson, The Hague,
The Netherlands,
September – October 1996;
Sotheby's, London, October
1996; Sotheby's, New York,
November 1996.

S.W.P.

Made less than two years after the *Circumcision* plate (cat. no. 1), this portrait, long identified as recording the likeness of Rembrandt's mother, Neeltgen Willemsdr. van Zuytbrouck, aged about sixty, shows an astonishing advancement in sensitivity and control of the medium. Famous even in the seventeenth century for his skill at painting the crisscrossing wrinkles and translucent skin of the aged,[1] Rembrandt here brings those same powers of observation to etching, creating a living likeness of an old woman with a web of wispy lines. The drypoint burr on the heavy black strokes near the breast of the figure means that this impression is probably early enough that Rembrandt's lightest marks in the plate are still visible – for example, the tiny scratches in the irises of the eyes which give the impression that they are light-colored.

The 1628 etching, a traditional three-quarter bust, is squarely in the realm of portraiture. In 1631, Rembrandt etched an intermediary piece, a three-quarter bust of his mother in black dress and veil (possibly mourning garb, as Rembrandt's father died in April 1630) in which her gaze is downcast and her lips pursed apparently in sadness. By 1633, in a second portrait in the exhibition (cat. no. 11) that shows Rembrandt's mother aged about sixty-five, the mourning garb is replaced with a light-colored, fringed headscarf. The eyes still look down, but the emotional affect is more neutral, and Rembrandt seems more interested in the simple practice of recording an old woman looking down.

A.C.W.

---

1 Julia Lloyd Williams, et al., *Rembrandt's Women*.
Edinburgh: National Gallery of Scotland, 2001, p. 66.

2

3 *The presentation in the temple with the angel: small plate*

1630
Etching.
Bartsch 51; Biörklund-Barnard 30-C ii/ii; Hind 18 ii/ii; Münz 191 ii/ii; Nowell-Usticke 51 i/i;
Ritman 29 ii/ii; Seidlitz 51 ii/ii; White-Boon 51 ii/ii.

PLATEMARK:
103 × 77 mm.

SHEET:
158–161 × 131–128 mm.

INSCRIPTION ON PLATE:
R L 1630, at lower center.

INSCRIPTIONS AND MARKS
ON SHEET:
On verso: stamp of S. W.
Pelletier [reddish-brown
ink] (2000.8.2.11); *Joseph R.
Ritman/cat. no. 29 (1995)*
[graphite]; *#201 Slg. W.
Mertens* [graphite]; *B.51,
Seidl. II. H.18 II. 7677*
[graphite]; *14759* [graphite,
upside down].

WATERMARK:
Fragment of Lily in a
Shield, with letter *BA*.

PROVENANCE:
Edouard Veltman, Bussum,
The Netherlands (not in
Lugt); [C. G. Boerner,
Leipzig, 1942, cat. 205,
lot 254]; Wilhelm Mertens,
Leipzig & Frankfurt (not in
Lugt); [Kornfeld & Klip-
stein, Auktion 122, June 14,
1967, lot 262] to [C. G.
Boerner, Düsseldorf];
[C. G. Boerner, Düsseldorf]
to private German collector
in 1967; repurchased by
[C. G. Boerner, Düsseldorf]
in 1984; sold to Joseph R.
Ritman in 1984. Joseph R.
Ritman, Amsterdam (not in
Lugt), cat. 1995, no. 29;
C. G. Boerner Inc., New
York.

DESCRIPTION:
An early, sharp impression
in black ink on ivory, laid
paper. With burr on the chin
of the standing figure of
Anna and on the left fore-
arm of the sitting priest.

This impression has all the
marks of being very early,
with sharp edges and a
remarkable depth of tone for
a pure etching of this date.
The impact of the impres-
sion is helped by the bright,
unpressed sheet of paper
with its large margins.

LITERATURE:
Graphik alter Meister (Ver-
steigerungs Katalog 205),
Leipzig: C. G. Boerner,
February 18, 1942, lot 254
(illustrated in pl. 14;
*Brillanter, früher Abdruck
…Ein köstliches, tadellos
frisches Exemplar mit 25–
30 mm breitem Papierrand,
wie es kaum je vorkommt*);
*Graphik und Handzeichnungen
alter Meister*. Bern: Kornfeld
und Klipstein (Auktion 122),
June 14, 1967, lot 262 (*ein
prachtvolles Exemplar in bezug
auf Druckqualität und Erhaltung….Sehr selten so schön*);
*A Collection of Etchings by
Rembrandt Harmensz. van
Rijn (1606–1669) formed by
Joseph R. Ritman*. London:
Artemis and Sotheby's
[1995], no. 29 (illustrated;
*It has all the signs of being very
early, with sharp edges and a
remarkable depth of tone for a
pure etching of this date*).

EXHIBITED:
Graphik alter Meister. Berlin:
C. G. Boerner, February 4–
7, 1942; *Graphik alter Meister*.
Leipzig: C. G. Boerner,
February 16–17, 1942;
Mees Pierson, The Hague,
The Netherlands,
September–October 1996;
Sotheby's, London, October
1996; Sotheby's New York,
November 1996.

S.W.P.

In this tiny print Rembrandt demonstrates an amazing ability to evoke the cavernous space of the temple within the confines of a small scrap of paper.[1] The scene is strictly divided between light at the left and shadow at the right, but in both areas the thunderous stone architecture of the temple is palpably conveyed. The figures lit by the streaming brilliance from the left include the infant Christ, resting in the arms of the aged Simeon, who according to the New Testament book of Luke had been told by the Holy Spirit that he would not die until he had seen the Messiah. Recognizing Christ, and knowing that his own time on earth is now complete, Simeon sings a hymn of praise to God and raises his hand in benediction of Christ and of Mary, who kneels before him. An angel – seemingly plucked from a Venetian painting – sweeps into the scene. His index finger is extended in a gesture that points out Christ as the chosen one to the startled prophetess Anna whom he addresses, and that also selects Simeon to be carried off to his reward.

The story of Simeon would have been both a timely and a poignant one for Rembrandt, whose father died in April 1630, the year in which this print was made. That Rembrandt may have intended this depiction of Simeon's hymn of praise as a memory of his father is suggested by his inclusion of what may be a portrait of Rembrandt's widowed mother, a shadowed figure dressed in

---

1 *Rembrandt Beyond the Brush: Master Prints from the Weil Collection*. Montgomery, Alabama: Montgomery Museum of Fine Arts, 1999, p. 21.

3

black with a black veil over her head, kneeling at Simeon's side. This portrait head is virtually identical to two etchings Rembrandt made of his mother in 1631 (White-Boon 343 and 349).

The figures on the stairs above, kneeling in supplication around the figure of the high priest, are cast in shadow, signifying that they are placing their trust in the wrong spiritual leader, while the unlikely but true king is at the foot of the staircase in the form of a lowly infant. Rembrandt communicates Christ's dominion over people of all ages and social stations through the figure of a Callot-esque beggar with a peg leg who retreats out of the composition, and by the remarkable little girl, bathed in light, who looks calmly out at the viewer (or perhaps at the beggar), tying us through her knowing gaze to the miracle of Christ's coming.

The heavy curtain at the top of the stairs adds to the dramatic shadow of that side of the composition, but in this narrative in which Christ makes his first entry into the temple, the curtain also foreshadows the portent that accompanied Christ's final agony of death on the cross, when, as stated in Matthew 27:51, "behold, the curtain of the temple was torn in two, from top to bottom."
A.C.W.

4 *The circumcision: small plate*

About 1630
Etching, with touches of drypoint.
Bartsch 48; Biörklund-Barnard 30-8 only state; Hind 19 only state; Münz 194 only state; Nowell-Usticke 48 only state; Ritman 26 ii/ii.[1]; Seidlitz 48 only state; White-Boon 48 only state.

PLATEMARK:
90 × 64 mm.

SHEET:
91 × 65 mm.

INSCRIPTION ON PLATE:
None.

INSCRIPTIONS AND MARKS ON SHEET:
On verso: *Joseph R. Ritman/cat. no. 26 (1995)* [graphite]; stamp of S. W. Pelletier [reddish-brown ink] (2000.8.2.10); *B48; B.48; 65* [graphite]; stamp of Marsden Jasael Perry [brown ink, very faint]; stamp of Heneage Finch, 5th Earl of Aylesford [black ink]; stamp of Ambroise Firmin-Didot [black ink]; *L 48* [graphite].

WATERMARK:
Arms of Strasbourg, with pendant letters *BA.*

PROVENANCE:
Heneage Finch, 5th Earl of Aylesford, London (Lugt 58) sold to Samuel Woodburn, London in 1846; [Samuel Woodburn, London]; Ambroise Firmin-Didot, Paris (Lugt 119), his sale, Paris, April 16 – May 12, 1877, lot 777 [G. Pawlowski, M. Danlos, Delisle]; Dr. August Sträter, Aix-la-Chapelle (cf. Lugt 787), his sale, Stuttgart, May 10–14, 1898, lot 680 [H. G. Gutekunst]; Marsden Jasael Perry, Providence, RI (Lugt 1880), his sale, Stuttgart, May 18–23, 1908, lot 1148 [H. G. Gutekunst]; Gustav von Róth, Krefeld, Germany (cf. Lugt 2772) to [C. G. Boerner, Düsseldorf, April 1979]; [C. G. Boerner, Düsseldorf, 1979, Neue Lagerliste Nr. 71, lot 37]; [C. G. Boerner, Düsseldorf, 1987, Neue Lagerliste Nr. 88, no. 36]; [C. G. Boerner, Düsseldorf, 1990, Neue Lagerliste Nr. 95, lot 36] to Joseph R. Ritman, Amsterdam, October 1990; Joseph R. Ritman, Amsterdam (not in Lugt), cat. 1995, no. 26; [C. G. Boerner Inc., New York, August 2, 2000].

DESCRIPTION:
An exceptional, strong, rich impression in black ink on ivory, laid paper. With burr on the mouth, along the head, and along the right shoulder, arm, and hand of the Christ child. Also with burr on the top of the hat of the priest standing at the left and along the head and right shoulder of the priest who holds the Christ child.

LITERATURE:
Manuscript catalogue of the Aylesford Collection. London: British Museum, no. 47.

Catalogue Illustré des Dessins et Estampes Composant la Collection de M. Ambroise Firmin-Didot. Paris: G. Pawlowski, M. Danlos und Delisle, April 16 – May 12, 1877, lot 777 (*Superbe épreuve*).

Katalog der berühmten Sammlung von Kupferstichen Radierungen Holzschnitten

This dynamic little print from the early 1630s shows the young Rembrandt at his most dramatic. The screaming Christ child, the flowing robes, the circle of quiet, pious adults, the magisterial priest behind, the spume of smoke, and, most of all, the powerful rush of space from the steps in front to the vault behind work together to create a scene of urgency and excitement out of a staid, formal ritual. This conception of the Christ child is radically different from the one we see more than twenty years later, when the circumcision takes place in the stable (cat. no. 30).

F.W.R.

---

1 In the exhibition catalogue of the Dutuit Collection (Musée du Petit Palais, Paris, 1986, no. 12), the author describes a previously unrecorded first state of the print before much additional shading in the background has been added. Both first and second states are illustrated.

4

und Zeichnungen des verstor-benen Herrn Dr. August Straeter in Aachen. Stuttgart: H. G. Gutekunst, May 14, 1898, lot 680 (*Brillanter Abdruck mit Rändchen*). *Aus Unseren Mappen Die Schönsten Neuerwerbungen 1979.* (Neue Lagerliste Nr. 71). Düsseldorf: C. G. Boerner, 1979, no. 37 (illustrated; *ungewöhnlich schöne Abzug*).

Gedruckte Kunst von Schongauer bis Goya (Neue Lagerliste Nr. 88), Düsseldorf: C. G. Boerner, 1987, no. 36 (illustrated; *ungewöhnlich schöne Abzug*).

Von Altdorfer bis Tiepolo Druckgraphik aus drei Jahrhunderten (Neue Lagerliste Nr. 95). Düsseldorf: C. G. Boerner, 1990, no. 36 (illustrated; *ungewöhnlich schöne Abzug*).

Katalog der umfangreichen und wertvollen Sammlungen der Herren Marsden J. Perry in Providence, RI (Amerika) und Fritz Rumpf in Potsdam. Stuttgart: H. G. Gutekunst, May 18, 1908, lot 1148 (*Prachtvoller Abdruck mit Rändchen*).

A Collection of Etchings by Rembrandt Harmensz. van Rijn (1606–1669) formed by Joseph R. Ritman. London: Artemis and Sotheby's [1995], no. 26 (illustrated). (*An exceptional, strong but subtle impression of this rather rare print, with very visible traces of burr on the central figure of the priest and the Christ child.*)

Clifford S. Ackley, *Rembrandt's Journey: Painter, Draftsman, Etcher.* Boston: Museum of Fine Arts, 2003, pp. 102, 314 (illustrated on p. 102, cat. no. 36).

EXHIBITED:

Aus Unseren Mappen Die Schönsten Neuerwerbungen 1979. Düsseldorf: C. G. Boerner, November 8–28, 1979.

Gedruckte Kunst von Schongauer bis Goya. Düsseldorf: C. G. Boerner, December 1–20, 1987.

Von Altdorfer bis Tiepolo Druckgraphik aus drei Jahrhunderten. Düsseldorf: C. G. Boerner, September 14 – October 5, 1990.

Mees Pierson, The Hague, The Netherlands, September – October 1996.

Sotheby's, London, October 1996.

Sotheby's New York, November 1996.

Rembrandt's Journey: Painter, Draftsman, Etcher. Boston: Museum of Fine Arts, October 26, 2003 – January 18, 2004.

Rembrandt's Journey: Painter, Draftsman, Etcher. Chicago: The Art Institute of Chicago, February 14 – May 9, 2004.

S.W.P.

4 150%

5 *Elderly couple behind a bank*

About 1630
Etching on ivory laid paper.
Bartsch 165; Biörklund-Barnard 30-5 iv/x; White-Boon 165 iv/x.

PLATEMARK:
111 × 81 mm.

SHEET:
111.5 × 81.5 mm.

INSCRIPTION ON PLATE:
RHL, faintly visible in the
lower right corner.

INSCRIPTIONS ON VERSO:
no. 158 / ni nom ni année
[brown ink]; *B. 165 / C. 162
/ avec le R a bas a / droite*
[graphite].

PROVENANCE:
Emile Galichon, Paris
(L. 856, on verso); B. Fred
Bianchi (stamp on verso)
Kornfeld & Klipstein, Bern,
Auktion, June 14, 1967,
catalogue 122, lot 275.

S.W.P.

This elderly couple behind a bank (or a gnarled tree trunk) is often incorrectly described as beggars. The woman, however, carries a basket, and a purse dangles from her waist. Nevertheless, age has taken its toll on her face and body, as it has on her companion, whose head is swathed in a bandage.

Although Dutch and earlier, Netherlandish artists were far from the only ones to address the old and the poor – Jacques Callot comes immediately to mind – they are the ones to look long and hard, and there are many of them. The taste for such pictures seems a mixture of curiosity, condescension, humor, and fear, judging by some of the inscriptions on the prints themselves. Nevertheless, at their best – in Pieter Brueghel, Adriaen van Ostade, or Rembrandt – poverty, old age, and sickness have not diminished their energy or individuality, as we see here in this raw and shocking image.

F.W.R.

5

6 *Man in a coat and fur cap leaning against a bank*

About 1630
Etching with touches of drypoint.
Bartsch 151; Biörklund-Barnard 30-6 i/iii; Hind 14 only state; Münz 109 i/ii; Nowell-Usticke 151 i/iii; Ritman 74 i/ii; Seidlitz 151 i/iii; White-Boon 151 i/iii.

PLATEMARK:
112 × 79 mm.

SHEET:
115 × 81.5 mm.

INSCRIPTION ON PLATE:
RHL in reverse in the upper right corner.

INSCRIPTIONS AND MARKS ON SHEET:
On verso: stamp of S. W. Pelletier [reddish-brown ink] (2003.10.6.10); 27 [graphite]; ___6 [graphite].

PROVENANCE:
Private collection, France, from a collection of Rembrandt etchings probably assembled in the eighteenth century; sale London, December 6, 1990, lot 132 [Sotheby's] to C. G. Boerner, Düsseldorf; sold to Joseph R. Ritman, Amsterdam in 1991 (not in Lugt); Artemis Fine Arts Inc., New York, October 6, 2003, invoice #157, #17639-74.

DESCRIPTION:
An excellent, early impression of the first state on ivory, laid paper with light plate tone. With burr on the man's beard and on the monogram (suggesting that Rembrandt scratched his signature directly onto the plate, in drypoint); with very fine lines of shading, sloping downward from left to right, to the right of the man's body and many fine horizontal scratches in the left background, all indications of an early impression of the first state.

LITERATURE:
Old Master Prints. London: Sotheby's, December 6, 1990, lot 32 (illustrated; *a very fine impression of the first state of three*).

A Collection of Etchings by Rembrandt Harmensz. van Rijn (1606–1669) formed by Joseph R. Ritman. London: Artemis and Sotheby's [1995], no. 74 (illustrated; *An exceptionally early impression. There is even burr on some of the lines, notably the monogram in the upper right corner*).

EXHIBITED:
Old Master Prints. London: Sotheby's, December 2–5, 1990.

Mees Pierson, The Hague, The Netherlands, September – October 1996.

Sotheby's, London, October 1996.

Sotheby's, New York, November 1996.

S.W.P.

Like most of Rembrandt's genre figures that lean on sticks, this print is inspired by the 1622 beggar etchings of Jacques Callot, of which Rembrandt owned a set. And it is only early impressions like this first state – so early that there is still drypoint burr on Rembrandt's monogram – that show the boldness of the hatching that is in part an evocation of Callot's linear etching style. However, the embroidered hem of the man's cape and his fur cap, and also his quite contented expression, argue that this man is not a beggar, but perhaps an old gentleman enjoying a break from his stroll and the warmth of the sun on his face.

A.C.W.

6

7 *Peasant with his hands behind his back*

1631
Etching with touches of burin.
Bartsch 135; Biörklund-Barnard 31-M iv/iv; Hind 69 iv/iv; Münz 290 iv/iv; Nowell-Usticke 135 v/v; Ritman 69 iv/iv;
Seidlitz 135 iv/iv; White-Boon 135 iv/iv.

PLATEMARK:
60 × 50 mm.

SHEET:
80 × 68.5 mm.

INSCRIPTION ON PLATE:
R–L 1631 in upper
left corner.

INSCRIPTIONS AND
MARKS ON SHEET:
On recto: at lower right:
stamp of George Hibbert;
13[?]4 [Gersaint no.];
initial *H.* On verso: initials
of John Barnard [brown
ink]; stamp of S. W. Pelletier
[reddish-brown ink] (1998;
12.11.34); *B135 iv; c.13227;
Joseph R. Ritman/Cat. No. 69
(1995)* [graphite]; *c 22348;
51; 3 imp MC* [graphite].

PROVENANCE:
John Barnard, London
(Lugt 1419, on verso), sale:
London, April 16 – May 16,
1798, lot 179 [Thomas
Philipe]; George Hibbert,
London (Lugt 2849, on
recto), sale: April 17 and
following days, 1809, lot
not identifiable, perhaps
no. 121 [Thomas Philipe];
Joseph R. Ritman, Amster-
dam (not in Lugt), cat. 1995,
no. 69; Artemis SA –
Luxembourg-Succursale de
Genève, invoice #99/0019,
December 11, 1998.

DESCRIPTION:
A very fine and sharp
impression in black ink on
ivory laid paper, printed
with light plate tone and
inky plate edges. With wide
margins. Nowell-Usticke
lists this print's rarity as
RRR⁻ (extremely rare).

LITERATURE:
*Catalogue of the Superb and
Entire Collection of Prints,
and Books of Prints, of John
Barnard, Esq.* London:
Thomas Philipe, April 16 –
May 16, 1798, lot 179.

George Hibbert Sale.
London: Thomas Philipe,
April 17, 1809 and follow-
ing days, no. 121 (?).

*A Collection of Etchings by
Rembrandt Harmensz. van
Rijn (1606–1669) formed by
Joseph R. Ritman.* London:
Artemis and Sotheby's
[1995], no. 69 (illustrated;
*A very fine and sharp impres-
sion presented with tone*).

EXHIBITED:
Mees Pierson, The Hague,
The Netherlands,
September – October 1996.

Sotheby's, London,
October 1996.

Sotheby's, New York,
November 1996.

S.W.P.

7

8 *Head of a man in a high cap*

About 1631
Etching on cream laid paper with inky plate edges.
Bartsch 302; White-Boon 302 iii/iii.

PLATEMARK:
37 × 22.5 mm.

SHEET:
40 × 26 mm.

INSCRIPTION ON PLATE:
none.

PROVENANCE:
Paul Davidsohn, Berlin (L. 654); Craddock & Barnard, London, June 15, 1970.

S.W.P.

9 *Grotesque profile: man in a high cap*

About 1631
Etching on ivory laid paper.
Bartsch 326; White-Boon 326 ii/iv.

PLATEMARK:
38.5 × 25.5 mm

SHEET:
38.5 × 25.5.

INSCRIPTION ON PLATE:
none.

PROVENANCE:
Duke of Buccleugh (L. 402, on verso); Paul Davidsohn (L. 654, on verso); Craddock & Barnard, London, June 15, 1970.

S.W.P.

9

8 200%

9 200%

10 *The small lion hunt (with two lions)*

About 1632
Etching.
Bartsch 115; Biörklund-Barnard 41-3 ii/ii; Hind 180 ii/ii; Münz 252 ii/ii; Nowell-Usticke 115 ii/ii; Ritman 65 ii/ii; Seidlitz 115 ii/ii; White-Boon 115 only state.

PLATEMARK:
154 × 121 mm.

SHEET:
157 × 124 mm.

INSCRIPTIONS ON PLATE:
none.

INSCRIPTIONS AND
MARKS ON SHEET:
On verso: *Viscount Downe London sale / December 7, 1972, lot 236* [graphite]; *Joseph R. Ritman / cat. no. 65 (1995)* [graphite]; S. W. Pelletier [reddish-brown ink] (2000.8.2.12); *Rembrandt Lion Hunt / B.115 / Bl. 87 / D 113* [graphite]; *P. mariette 1661* [brown ink]; stamp of L. Lancy [red ink]; *781* [graphite]; stamp of Marsden Jasael Perry [brown ink, faint]; *B. No 115 tres rare* [graphite]; *B. 115. No 115. tres rare* [graphite] *C. M* [graphite].

PROVENANCE:
Pierre Mariette (Lugt 1789); Marsden Jasael Perry, Providence, RI (Lugt 1880), his sale, Stuttgart, May 18–23, 1908, lot 1214 [H. G. Gutekunst]; C. F. G. R. Schwerdt, his sale, London, June 20, 1939, lot 940 [Sotheby's]; Viscount Downe, Wykeham Abbey, Scarborough (cf. Lugt 719ª), his sale, London, December 7, 1972 (Part II), lot 236 [Sotheby's]; Dr. Leslie E. Lancy, Ellwood City, PA (not in Lugt) to

C. G. Boerner, Düsseldorf; C. G. Boerner, Düsseldorf to Joseph R. Ritman, 1985; Joseph R. Ritman, Amsterdam (not in Lugt), cat. 1995, no. 65; C. G. Boerner Inc., New York, August 2, 2000, invoice #194.

DESCRIPTION:
An early, rich impression in black ink, with plate tone and fine plate polishing scratches, on ivory, laid paper. In state i (156 × 126 mm.), the plate edges are irregular and inky and the background is dirty. The farthest right point of the left back paw of the lioness is about 3 mm. from the right platemark. In state ii, the plate edges are trimmed (154 × 121 mm.), the corners are rounded and the plate edges are cleaned. The distance between the paw of the lioness and the right platemark is now 1 mm.

The sense of rapid movement of the animals is vividly suggested. Rembrandt has bitten the foreground and the horseman at the left very deeply in order to help frame the subject, while the lions in the background are lightly etched.

This impression was in P. Mariette's collection during Rembrandt's lifetime.

This is one of two lion hunt pictures that Rembrandt made in his twenties. The first, in 1629, was among Rembrandt's first forays into genre subjects as he learned the art of etching, and was undoubtedly inspired by a print in his own collection, a lion hunt by the sixteenth-century Italian engraver Antonio Tempesta.[1] Expanding on his *Small Lion Hunt (with one Lion)*, Rembrandt not only adds a lion but shows the tremendous improvement in his skill as a printmaker in only two or three years. Not only are the rearing horse and its rider in shadow more expertly contrasted with the background, but through the use of different depths of biting Rembrandt convincingly conveys the foreground, the middle ground (in which the lioness attacks a man) and the distant background that shows us the rest of the hunting procession in a

---

1 Christopher White, *Rembrandt as an Etcher*. New Haven: Yale University Press, 1999, p. 171.

10

LITERATURE:

Katalog der umfangreichen und wertvollen Sammlungen der Herren Marsden J. Perry in Providence, RI (Amerika) und Fritz Rumpf in Potsdam enthaltend die Werke von Dürer und Rembrandt. Stuttgart: H. G. Gutekunst, May 18–23, 1908, lot 1214 (*Prachtvoller Abdruck mit Rand und mit der Signatur, von Mariette*).

The Schwerdt Collection. Catalogue of the Renowned Collection of Books, Manuscripts, Prints & Drawings relating to Hunting, Hawking & Shooting, formed by the late C. F. G. R. Schwerdt, Esq. London: Sotheby & Co., June 20, 1939, lot 940.

The Viscount Downe Collection of Rembrandt Etchings. Part Two. London: Sotheby & Co., December 7, 1972, lot 236 (illustrated; *A very fine, early impression showing strongly the scratches on the plate which were later burnished clean*).

A Collection of Etchings by Rembrandt Harmensz. van Rijn (1606–1669) formed by Joseph R. Ritman. London: Artemis and Sotheby's [1995], no. 65 (illustrated).

EXHIBITED:

Mees Pierson, The Hague, The Netherlands, September – October 1996.

Sotheby's, London, October 1996.

Sotheby's, New York, November 1996.

S.W.P.

deftly indicated landscape. He achieves all of this without sacrificing any of the spontaneous, turbulent energy of the fight and without diminishing the beasts' ferocity. It should also be noted that when Rembrandt made this etching, he had never actually seen a real lion, as he did later in his life in traveling circuses, recording them in several masterful drawings. Here, Rembrandt clearly does not yet understand how to depict the mane of the male lion crouching at center.

A.C.W.

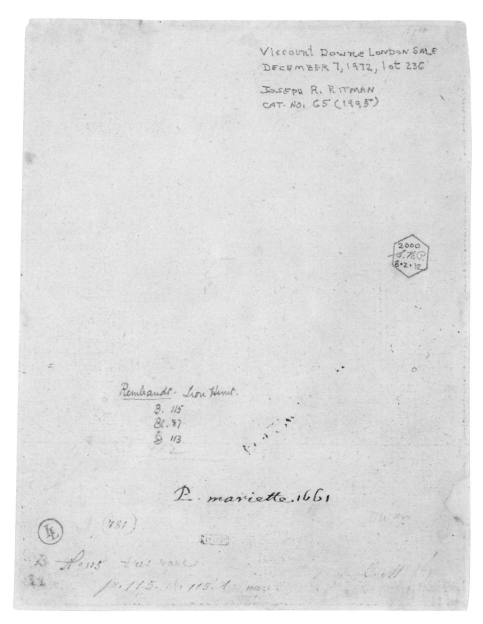

Rembrandt. Lion Hunt.
B. 115
Bl. 87
H. 113

P. mariette. 1661

(781)

10 verso

11 *The artist's mother in a cloth headdress, looking down: head only*

1633
Etching.
Bartsch 351; Biörklund-Barnard 33-F ii/ii; Hind 107 ii/iii; Münz 87 ii/iii;
Nowell-Usticke 351 i/ii; Seidlitz 351 ii/iii; White-Boon 351 ii/ii.

PLATEMARK:
42–41.5 × 41 mm.

SHEET:
42–43 × 42 mm.

INSCRIPTION ON PLATE:
Rembrandt f. 1633 at
upper center.

INSCRIPTION AND
MARKS ON SHEET:
On verso: *15/260*; *B. 351*;
15–; stamp of S. W.
Pelletier [reddish–brown
ink] (1999; 11.11.16).

PROVENANCE:
Swann Galleries, Inc.,
New York, sale 1840,
November 11, 1999, lot 119.

DESCRIPTION:
A rich, early impression of
the second state in black ink
on ivory, laid paper, after
reduction of the plate size.
With plate tone and inky
plate edges.

LITERATURE:
Works of Art on Paper. New
York: Swann Galleries, Inc.,
November 11, 1999, lot 119
(illustrated).

EXHIBITED:
Works of Art on Paper. New
York: Swann Galleries Inc.,
November 6–10, 1999.

S.W.P.

See entry for cat. no. 2, page 46.

11

12 *Joseph's coat brought to Jacob*

About 1633
Etching with touches of drypoint.
Bartsch 38; Biörklund-Barnard 33-I i/ii; Hind 104 i/ii; Münz 172 i/ii; Nowell-Usticke 38 i/iv;
Ritman 17 i/ii; Seidlitz 38 i/ii; White-Boon 38 i/ii.

PLATEMARK:
108 × 80 mm.

SHEET:
110 × 81 mm.

INSCRIPTION ON PLATE:
Rembrandt / van. Rijn. fe. at
lower right.

INSCRIPTIONS AND
MARKS ON SHEET:
On recto: stamp of George
Hibbert [black ink]; stamp
of Joseph Maberly [black
ink]. On verso: stamp of S.
W. Pelletier [reddish-brown
ink] (2003.10.6.9); stamp of
Marsden Jasael Perry [black
ink]; *9? 12* [graphite];
N⁰ 72 [brown ink].

WATERMARK:
*Fleur-de-lis in Small Crowned
Shield. (Strasbourg Lily.)*

PROVENANCE:
George Hibbert, London
(Lugt 2849, on recto), sale:
London, April 17 and fol-
lowing days, 1809, lot 27
[Thomas Philipe]; Joseph
Maberly, London (Lugt
1845, on recto), sale:
London, May 14 and fol-
lowing days, 1851, lot 471
[Sotheby's]; Marsden Jasael
Perry, Providence, RI (Lugt
1880; on verso, faint), sale:
Stuttgart, May 18–29, 1908,
lot 1136 [H. G. Gutekunst];
Sotheby Parke-Bernet Inc.,
November 13–15, 1980, lot
987; Paul McCarron Fine
Prints and Drawings, New
York, 1981 catalogue, lot 11,
sold to Artemis Fine Arts
Ltd., London, sold to Joseph
R. Ritman, Amsterdam,
1982 (not in Lugt); Artemis
Fine Arts Inc., New York,
October 6, 2003, invoice
#157, # 17639–17.

DESCRIPTION:
A brilliant impression of the
first state of two, in black ink
on ivory, laid paper, printed
with plate tone. There is
drypoint burr on the sleeve
and cuff of the pointing
man and also a second faint
outline of his thumb, below
and longer than the upper
one, a feature that disappears in later impressions.

LITERATURE:
*Catalogue of a Superb Assem-
blage of Prints and Books of
Prints, formed by a Gentleman of Distinguished Taste.*
[George Hibbert]. London:
Thomas Philipe, April 17,
1809 and following days,
lot 27 (BRILLIANT).

*Catalogue of the Entire and
Very Choice Collection of
Engravers, the Property of
Joseph Maberly, Esq.* London:
S. Leigh Sotheby & John
Wilkinson, May 26 – June 9,
1851, lot 471 (*a remarkably
brilliant impression from Mr.
Hibbert's collection*).

*Katalog der umfangreichen
und wertvollen Sammlungen
der Herren Marsden J. Perry
in Providence, RI (Amerika)
und Fritz Rumpf in Potsdam
enthaltend die Werke von
Dürer und Rembrandt.*
Stuttgart: H. G. Gutekunst,
May 18–23, 1908, lot 1136
(*Prachtvoller früher Abdruck
mit Rändchen*).

*Nineteenth and Twentieth
Century Prints. Old Master
Prints.* New York: Sotheby
Parke-Bernet Inc., Novem-
ber 13–15, 1980, lot 987
(illustrated).

After growing jealous of Joseph for his dreams and visions (the subject of catalogue number 18), Joseph's brothers abducted him and sold him into slavery in Egypt. To trick their father Jacob, they dipped Joseph's coat in goat's blood and brought it to him, with the story that Joseph had been devoured by a wild animal. Here Jacob recoils in grief and dismay as one of the brothers, his face shadowed to show his villainy, tells the lie. The purse of the kneeling brother bulges with money, reminding us that Joseph's brothers had just sold him to the Ishmaelites for twenty pieces of silver – which is significant in this story that prefigures Christ's passion because Christ was also sold – betrayed – by his disciple Judas for a blood price of silver coins. Rembrandt's hirsute self-portrait in the brother at the exact center of the composition (contrasted with the bald brother next to him) indi-cates his familiarity with human weakness.

This is a superb early impression from the plate in which an abandoned attempt at the thumb of the pointing brother still prints, and the fine details of the landscape and two travelers in the background are still clearly visible. Rembrandt's penchant for lavishing great care on seemingly unimportant details manifests itself in the door of the house, with its convincing texture of weathered wood and the palpable impression of its weight pulling on the cast-iron hinges. Rembrandt seems to wish to present simultaneously the dramatic biblical narrative in all its emotional complexity, and to make that narrative vivid and real by bring-ing to life the physical environment in which it takes place.

A.C.W.

16th and 17th Century Masters. New York: Paul McCarron Fine Prints and Drawings by Old and Modern Masters, 1981, p. 7, lot 11 (illustrated; *A fine, richly inked impression with the lines printing clear, giving the print the appearance of an ink drawing*).

A Collection of Etchings by Rembrandt Harmensz. van Rijn (1606–1669) formed by Joseph R. Ritman. London: Artemis and Sotheby's [1995], no. 16 (illustrated).

EXHIBITED:
Nineteenth and Twentieth Century Prints. Old Master Prints. New York: Sotheby Parke Bernet Inc., November 8–12, 1980.

Mees Pierson, The Hague, The Netherlands, September – October 1996.

Sotheby's, London, October 1996.

Sotheby's, New York, November 1996.

S.W.P.

12

13 *Christ driving the money changers from the temple*

1635
Etching on thin, white laid paper.
Bartsch 69; White-Boon 69 ii/ii.

PLATEMARK:
137 × 169 mm.

SHEET:
139.5 × 170 mm.

INSCRIPTION ON PLATE:
Rembrandt f. 1635 at
lower right.

PROVENANCE:
Craddock & Barnard,
London; Associated
American Artists, New
York, August 23, 1965.

S.W.P.

This etching offers compelling evidence of Rembrandt's love of collecting prints and shows us that his own collection inspired him again and again in the creation of completely new works that still look back to important roots. In this case, the figure of Christ with the whip is taken verbatim from Dürer's woodcut Passion depiction of the same subject, albeit reversed (thereby making Christ, uniquely, left-handed). This print shows Rembrandt at the height of his High Baroque period; instead of the close quarters of Dürer's print, however, Rembrandt has enlarged the composition to a large interior reminiscent of Venetian painting,[1] showing us the enormous temple and all the variety of people that could be found there, with a full measure of humorous anecdotal detail thrown in, including a stampeding calf and an escaping pigeon. The gospels of Matthew, Mark, and John all record Christ's fury at the money changers and merchants doing their business in the temple; in Mark 11:17, he casts them out, accusing them of making the temple "a den of robbers."

Ever the master of foreshadowing, Rembrandt also refers to Mark 11:18, "and the scribes and the chief priests heard it, and they sought how they might destroy him." The uncharacteristic violence Christ exhibits in cleansing the temple is the act that sets in motion his passion and death; the authorities decide he simply can no longer be left to his own devices. Accordingly, one of the clerics or elders participating in the ceremony in the background looks back over his shoulder with an expression of concern at Christ's vigorous expulsion of the money changers.[2]

A.C.W.

1 Kenneth Clark, *Rembrandt and the Italian Renaissance*. New York: New York University Press, 1964, p. 104.

2 The meeting in the background right between the high priest and his surrounding elders and clerics and the kneeling youth has not been suitably explained. Is Rembrandt intending this scene as Christ Disputing with the Doctors in the Temple, i.e., depicting Christ as a child in the same scene with Christ the grown man?

13

14 *The stoning of St. Stephen*

1635
Etching with touches of drypoint.
Bartsch 97; Biörklund-Barnard 35-A i/ii; Hind 125 i/ii; Münz 205 i/ii;
Nowell-Usticke 97 i/iv; Seidlitz 97 i/ii; White-Boon 97 i/ii.

PLATEMARK:
94.5–95.0 × 85.5 mm.

SHEET:
95.5 x 86 mm.

INSCRIPTION ON PLATE:
Rembrandt f. 1635 in lower
left corner.

INSCRIPTIONS AND
MARKS ON SHEET:
On verso: stamp of S. W.
Pelletier [reddish-brown
ink] (2000.5.11.7).

PROVENANCE:
Venator & Hanstein KG,
Cologne, September 26,
1995, lot 2385; Swann Gal-
leries, New York, sale 1860,
May 11, 2000, lot 158.

DESCRIPTION:
A brilliant, early, toned
impression on ivory, laid
paper. With touches of burr
in the black spot above the
Saint's shoe, on the sash to
the right of the Saint's head,
along the nose of the man
holding the Saint's robe, and
on the Saint's right heel.
With strong, clear diagonal
rays in the background at
the upper right. In the
white area above and to the
right of the slipper there
are fine vertical polishing
scratches that extend up into
the lower part of the Saint's
robe and to the right of
the robe. With a fine, clear,
horizontal line directly
below the signature.

LITERATURE:
*Bücher. Manuskripte.
Autographen. Druckgraphik.
Handzeichnungen*
(Auktion 71). Cologne:
Venator & Hanstein K G,
September 25 and 26, 1995,
lot 2385 (incorrectly
described as a third state).

Works of Art on Paper.
New York: Swann Galleries.
May 11, 2000, lot 158
(illustrated).

EXHIBITED:
Works of Art on Paper. New
York: Swann Galleries Inc.,
May 6–10, 2000.

S.W.P.

As he so often did, Rembrandt here packs a dramatic biblical narrative into a very small space,
showing the martyrdom of St. Stephen outside the
city of Jerusalem. The deed takes place on a little
promontory above the city, the divine light from
above indicated with insistent slanting lines that
fall on the crown of the saint's head. But by isolat-
ing St. Stephen's slipper in the foreground, Rembrandt also makes a poignant statement about the
saint's death.

Rembrandt saw this same slipper in his good
friend Jan Lievens's etching of *St. Jerome in Peni-
tence* of 1631, which shows the hermit saint having kicked his slippers off presumably after a walk
in the wilderness; there, they are a symbol of the
saint's hard life of physical privation. Like the letter
"A" formed by the firewood in *Abraham's Sacrifice*
(cat. no. 31), or the cockle shell on the ground in
the "Hundred Guilder Print" (cat. no. 27), Rembrandt uses the cast-off slipper here to subtly comment on the main narrative. The empty slipper
makes the saint's bare foot more visible and more
real, more naked and vulnerable, thus emphasizing the fragility of his life and the injustice of
his murder.

A.C.W.

14

15 *The tribute money*

About 1635
Etching on ivory laid paper, with burr and inky plate edges.
Bartsch 68; White-Boon 68 i/ii.

PLATEMARK:
73 × 103 mm.

SHEET:
76 × 105.5 mm.

INSCRIPTIONS ON PLATE:
none.

PROVENANCE:
A.P.F. Robert-Dumesnil,
Paris (L. 2200, on recto);
Craddock & Barnard,
London, catalogue 117, no.
246, November 19, 1968.

S.W.P.

In a tradition that goes back in Rembrandt's cognizance at least to the engravings of Schongauer he owned, Rembrandt takes the opportunity of this biblical narrative to surround the perfect figure of Christ with a range of types whose boorish expressions show the imperfection of humanity. Rembrandt's love of oriental costume is seen in the ornate garb, caps, and turbans of the Pharisees that contrast with the simplicity of Christ's unadorned robe and overmantle.

The story of the tribute money is found in Matthew 22. A group of Pharisees, seeking to ensnare Jesus by getting him in trouble with the Roman authorities, test his allegiance to Rome by asking him if it is legal to pay taxes to Caesar. Asking them to show him a coin, Christ notes Caesar's likeness on it and instructs them therefore to "render to Caesar the things that are Caesar's and to God the things that are God's." In expression of this verse, Christ's left hand points to the Pharisee holding the coin; his right points up to heaven. This Pharisee – as he stares, confounded by the cleverness and wisdom of Christ's reply – presents the dour profile of a Roman coin portrait. In the middle ground at left, two men study a book; through this subtle gesture, Rembrandt underlines the basis for the scene in holy scripture.

A.C.W.

15

16 *Polander standing with arms folded*

About 1635
Etching on ivory laid paper with light plate tone.
Bartsch 140; Nowell-Usticke 140 ii/ii; White-Boon 140 only state.

PLATEMARK:
50 × 46 mm.

SHEET:
82 × 81 mm.

INSCRIPTIONS ON PLATE:
none.

PROVENANCE:
Baron J. G. Verstolk van
Soelen, Soelen, The Nether-
lands (cf. L. 2490), sale
Amsterdam, October 26
and following, 1847; A.P.F.
Robert-Dumesnil, Paris;
Neville D. Goldsmid
(L. 1962, on verso); Moscow
Museum duplicate
(N. 40753, on verso);
Nicolas Vassilievitch Basnine
(L. 1960, on verso);
Gutekunst & Klipstein,
Bern; Captain Gordon W.
Nowell-Usticke, Virgin
Islands, Parke-Bernet sale,
New York, May 1, 1968,
lot 357.

S.W.P.

The tiny and sensitively etched Polander belongs to Rembrandt's genre prints of lower class figures inspired by Jacques Callot's etchings of the 1620s. This print is also called the barrel-organ player, although the instrument that the figure cranks with his right hand is almost certainly a hurdy-gurdy, which is a stringed instrument. Callot and his earlier contemporary and countryman Jacques Bellange both made genre etchings of hurdy-gurdy players.

A.C.W.

16

16 200%

16 verso, 200%

17 *Young man in a velvet cap: Petrus Sylvius*

1637
Etching with touches of drypoint.
Bartsch 268; Biörklund-Barnard 37-C ii/ii; Hind 151 ii/ii; Münz 58 ii/ii; Nowell-Usticke 268 i;
Ritman 102 ii/ii; Seidlitz 268 ii/ii; White-Boon 268 ii/ii.

PLATEMARK:
96 × 83 mm.

SHEET:
170 × 136 mm.

INSCRIPTION ON PLATE:
Rembrandt / f 1637 in upper
left corner.

INSCRIPTIONS AND
MARKS ON SHEET:
On verso: stamp of Louis
Galichon [blue ink]; stamp
of S. W. Pelletier [reddish-
brown ink] (2002.2.12.1);
*Joseph R. Ritman / cat. no. 102
(1995)* [graphite]; stamp of
Atherton Curtis [black ink];
9078/9803 [C. G. Boerner,
Düsseldorf inventory nos.;
graphite, faint]; *?/ fine*
[graphite, very faint]; *B.268
Seidl.II* [graphite]; stamp of
Emile Galichon [black ink];
2211 [graphite]; *248./249*
[brown ink]; initials: *D. D.*
[pale brown ink]; initials:
TmW 1853 [brown ink];
Petrus Silvius [in seventeenth-
century hand, dark brown
ink]; *Petrus Silvius* [in
nineteenth-century hand,
brown ink].

WATERMARK:
Fragment of a shield with
initials *WR*, probably part
of the *Strasbourg Bend* or
Strasbourg Lily (see *Water-
marks in Rembrandt's Prints.*
Washington: National
Gallery of Art, 1998, pp.
173–177 and 190–198, nos.
35 and 36).

PROVENANCE:
Petrus Sylvius, Amsterdam
& Frise (1610–1652; his
signature, verso) [Petrus was
the son of Rembrandt's
friend, the clergyman
Johannes Cornelis Sylvius,
whose portrait was etched
twice by Rembrandt (Bartsch
266 and 280) and who was

the uncle and guardian of
Rembrandt's wife, Saskia];
Jan Pietersz. Zomer, Ams-
terdam (1641–1724; cf.
Lugt 1511), whose three
volumes of Rembrandt
etchings were purchased in
1720 by Antonio Maria
Zanetti, Vienna (1680–1767);
Zanetti's descendants sold
his Rembrandt prints in
1791 to Baron Dominique
Vivant-Denon; Baron
Dominique Vivant-Denon,
Paris (1747–1825; Lugt 738
on verso; cf. Lugt 779), sale:
Paris, February 12, 1827,
the three volumes of Rem-
brandt etchings were unsold;
the Baron's beneficiary, his
nephew, Monsieur Brunet-
Denon, sold the volumes
privately in 1829 to the
London dealer, Samuel
Woodburn, who dispersed
the etchings among several
English collectors; Thomas
Miller Whitehead, London,
1853; (1821–1897; Lugt 2449
and Suppl., on verso); Emile
Galichon, Paris (1829–1875;
Lugt 1058, on verso), sale:
Hôtel Drouet, Paris (expert
Clément), May 10, 1875, lot
563, sold to Louis Galichon,
Paris (1829–1893; Lugt 1060,
on verso); Atherton Curtis,
New York & Paris (1863–
1943; Lugt 94 and Suppl., on
verso), sale: Bern (Gutekunst
& Klipstein), April 28, 1955,
lot 116; private Argentinean
collector to C. G. Boerner,
Düsseldorf in June 1972; C.
G. Boerner, Düsseldorf,
Neue Lagerliste 62 (1973),
no. 40, sold to a private
German collector, who sold
it through Hauswedell &
Nolte, Hamburg, June 2,
1977, lot 143; purchased by
C. G. Boerner, Düsseldorf;
sold in 1979 to a private
collector, U.S.A.; Christie,

Although this is a masterfully executed and psy-
chologically complex portrait, and a magnificent
early impression of it to boot, the true significance of this specific impression in the Pelletier
collection is a simple inscription on the verso. For
decades, this print was believed to be a portrait of
Ferdinand Bol, one of Rembrandt's pupils. However, based on the name "Petrus Sylvius" written
on the verso of this impression in a seventeenth-
century hand, Dieuwke de Hoop Scheffer has
convincingly argued that the portrait records the
likeness of the son of the preacher Jan Cornelis
Sylvius, who was the guardian of Rembrandt's wife,
Saskia. The son, Petrus Sylvius, was trained as a pastor, like his father, and would have been twenty-
seven years old and newly called to a congregation
in Friesland in the north of the country when this
portrait was recorded. De Hoop Scheffer supposes
that it was made to commemorate the launching
of his ministry and as a keepsake for his family after
his departure.[1]

The *Young Man in a Velvet Cap* does not have
the polish, refinement, and wit of the carefully
orchestrated masterwork that is the portrait of
the preacher Cornelis Claesz. Anslo, on the cover
of this catalogue – but it succeeds much better as
a depiction of a human personality.[2] This likeness
ingeniously insinuates the personality of the sitter
rather than proclaiming his prominence. Rembrandt shows us a shy young man who has yet to

---

1 Dieuwke de Hoop Scheffer, "Petrus Sylvius par
Rembrandt," in *Liber Amicorum Karel G. Boon*, Amsterdam,
Swets & Zeitlinger BV, 1974, pp. 96–101.

2 As Prof. Pelletier mentions in his essay, Degas was deeply
influenced by this print; see, for example, his portrait of
Joseph Tourny, Delteil 4.

17

Manson & Woods Ltd., London sale, November 28, 1989, lot 101a to C. G. Boerner, Düsseldorf; to Joseph R. Ritman, Amsterdam, cat. 1995, no. 102; Artemis Fine Arts Ltd., London and Sotheby's London, (inventory no. 17338); C. G. Boerner, Inc., New York, (inventory no. 17639); sold to S. W. Pelletier, February 12, 2002.

DESCRIPTION:
A superb, early impression with delicate plate tone in black ink on ivory, laid paper. With deeply imprinted platemark and with burr on the drypoint touches in the hair, on the left eye, and on the lips and chin. There is a very faint vertical scratch, 14 mm. in length, above the cap just to the right of center; also there is a distinct, wavy, almost horizontal line, 10 mm. in length, starting just below the lower of two hairs and extending left from the sitter's right cheek; these scratches indicate an early impression. With 26–41 mm. margins.

This impression matches the description for state two in most recent catalogues of Rembrandt etchings. The unique impression of the so-called first state in Paris is regarded by G. W. Nowell-Usticke and Adrian Eeles of Artemis Fine Arts, London as a falsification. Thus, there appears to be a single state of this etching.

LITERATURE:
Catalogue D'Estampes Anciennes et Dessins composant La magnifique Collection de feu M. Emile Galichon. Hôtel Drouet, Paris: M. Clément, sale: March 10, 1875, lot 563. (*Magnifique épreuve du premier état, avec des parties claires dans les cheveux.*)

Kupferstiche, Radierungen und Holzschnitte Alter Meister. Bern: Gutekunst & Klipstein, April 28, 1955, lot 116. (*Prachtvoller früher Druck, von frischester Erhaltung…. Tiefschwarz, mit noch rauhen*

Plattenrändern, mit leichtem Ton gedruckt.)

Graphik alter Meister (Neue Lagerliste Nr. 62), Düsseldorf: C. G. Boerner, 1973, no. 40 (illustrated on recto and verso). (*Gewiss eines der volkommensten Exemplare, die von dieser Radierung erhalten sind, und durch seine Herkunft besonders hoch qualifiziert.*)

Dieuwke de Hoop Scheffer, "Petrus Sylvius par Rembrandt" in *Liber Amicorum Karel G. Boon.* Edited by Dieuwke de Hoop Scheffer, Carlos van Hasselt, Christopher White, Amsterdam: Swets & Zeitlinger BV, 1974, pp. 96–101 (illustrated on recto and verso).

Gemälde, Zeichungen und Graphik des 15.-19. Jahrhunderts (auktion 221). Hamburg: Dr. Ernst Hauswedell & Ernst Nolte, June 2, 1977, no. 143 (illustrated on cover). (*Prachtvolles Exemplar der schönen Porträtdarstellung, brillant im Druck u. von einwandfreier, frischer Erhaltung ….Durch Druckqualität, Volkommenheit der Erhaltung wie illustre Provenienz gleichermassen qualifizierte Exemplare dieser Radierung dürften von allergrösster Seltenheit sein.*)

Important Old Master Contemporary and Modern Prints. London: Christie, Manson & Woods Ltd., November 28, 1989, lot 101a (illustrated; *An excellent impression of this rare print*).

A Collection of Etchings by Rembrandt Harmensz. van Rijn (1606–1669) formed by Joseph R. Ritman. London: Artemis and Sotheby's [1995], no. 102 (illustrated; *The impression is rich, printed with tone and so early that it seems almost to have burr, even though no drypoint has been used. It must be one of the very first pulls*).

assert his place in society, who in spite of looking in our direction, still maintains an emotional distance from us. Unlike Anslo, Sylvius has no spacious desk, no paintings on the wall, only the corner of a small table at left on which his stacked books (or perhaps a single book open on a book rest) speak of his newly gained erudition. His moustache is sparse, and he does not quite inhabit the fine clothes, which are also a bit too big for him, and his sober expression is incongruous with the jaunty note of the velvet cap. All of these factors contribute to a convincing sense of emotional fragility that helps the print succeed beyond its modest frame.

A.C.W.

EXHIBITED:
D'Estampes Anciennes et Dessins, Hôtel Drouet, Paris, May 8–9, 1875.

Graphik alter Meister. Düsseldorf: C. G. Boerner, April 2–18, 1973.

Gemälde, Zeichnungen und Graphik des 15.-19. Jahrhunderts. Hamburg: Hauswedell & Nolte, May 24–27 and May 31 – June 1, 1977.

Important Old Master Contemporary and Modern Prints. London: Christie, Manson & Woods Ltd., November 23–27, 1989.

Mees Pierson, The Hague, The Netherlands, September – October 1996.

Sotheby's, London, October 1996.

Sotheby's New York, November 1996.

S.W.P.

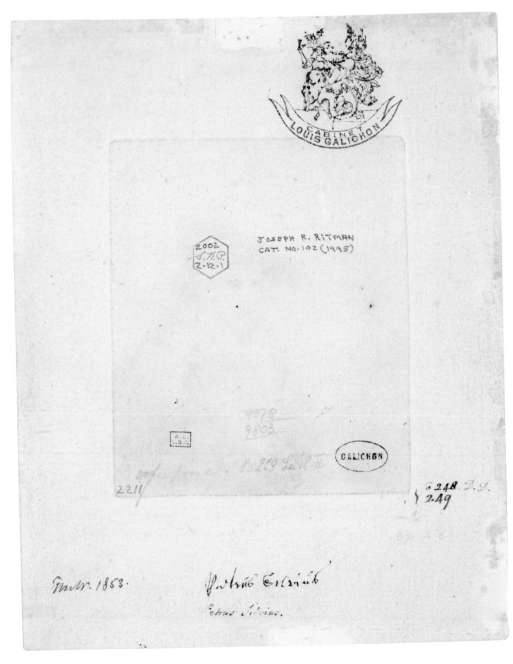

17 verso

18 *Joseph telling his dreams*

1638
Etching on ivory laid paper.
Bartsch 37; Biörklund-Barnard 38-E ii/iv; White-Boon 37 ii/iii.

PLATEMARK:
111 × 83 mm.

SHEET:
111 × 85 mm.

INSCRIPTION ON PLATE:
Rembrant [sic] *f. 1638* at
lower left on footwarmer.

PROVENANCE:
J. Camesina de Pomal,
Vienna (L. 429, on verso);
A. Artaria, Vienna (L. 33,
on verso); Artaria & Co.,
Vienna (L. 90, on verso);
George Biörklund, Stock-
holm (L. 1138ᶜ suppl. on
verso); Craddock & Barnard,
London, catalogue 112,
no. 114, July 8, 1966.

S.W.P.

Joseph was an Old Testament figure whose life was seen to foreshadow that of Christ, and indeed Rembrandt casts this scene as if he were depicting Christ among the doctors in the temple, which he etched three times. The scene is found in Genesis 37, in which the young Joseph reveals two dreams that foretell his future success. The etching appears to illustrate the second dream, in which Joseph sees a vision of the sun and the moon and eleven stars (his father, mother, and eleven brothers) bowing down to him. The ten envious brothers are depicted here, one only by his left hand on the table; Benjamin, the youngest, innocent brother, is appropriately absent. Joseph's father, Jacob, is seated at lower left, and his mother, Rachel, reclines on the bed, touching her brow pensively as she listens to her son.

Between 1631 and 1638, Rembrandt made at least three drawings and a grisaille on paper, working out the composition and the figures of Joseph, his parents, the turbaned figure above Joseph, and the seated woman with the book. This last figure was placed into the scene virtually unchanged from Rembrandt's drawing,[1] and because of her youth may be identified as Dinah, Jacob's only daughter.[2]

Joseph's large, broad hands, at the center of the composition, vividly communicate the act of storytelling and specifically a bowing-down motion associated with Joseph's vision. The fingers of Joseph's left hand extend toward Rachel's book, subtly pointing out that Joseph's dream will pass the ultimate test of veracity and become holy scripture. The faces of Joseph's brothers ranged all around him are studies of incredulity or incomprehension. A dog at Jacob's feet licks himself, further illustrating the ignorance of the brothers, who, like the dog, hear Joseph but cannot understand the ultimate significance of his dream.

A.C.W.

1 See Erik Hinterding,
Ger Luijten, and Martin
Royalton-Kisch, *Rembrandt
the Printmaker*, London:
British Museum, 2000,
pp. 160–161.

2 Clifford S. Ackley, et al.,
*Rembrandt's Journey: Painter,
Draftsman, Etcher*. Boston:
Museum of Fine Arts, 2003,
p. 122.

18

19 *Cornelis Claesz. Anslo, preacher*

1641
Etching and drypoint with burr on cream laid paper.
Bartsch 271; Biörklund-Barnard 41-J ii/iv; Nowell-Usticke 271 ii/vi; White-Boon 271 ii/ii.

PLATEMARK:
187 × 159 mm.

SHEET:
199–200 × 172 mm.

INSCRIPTION ON PLATE:
Rembrandt f. 1641 on object
near wall, center right.

PROVENANCE:
George Biörklund, Stockholm (L. 1138^c suppl. on verso); Craddock & Barnard, London, catalogue 115, no. 267, February 26, 1969.

S.W.P.

Rembrandt devoted unusually careful preparation to his portrait of Cornelis Claesz. Anslo (1592–1646), a cloth merchant and preacher in the Waterland Congregation, a sect of the Mennonite brotherhood. In 1640, Rembrandt made two different preparatory drawings for the etching (now in the British Museum and the Louvre); the one he chose shows evidence of having been transferred directly to the plate. In 1641, Rembrandt also made a masterful painted portrait of Anslo and his wife, now in Berlin.

Rembrandt brings to this portrait etching a supreme painterly polish, rendering the surfaces and textures of the felt hat, the starched ruff, and especially the fur-trimmed mantle. Through these details, in the context of the capitalist economy of the United Provinces, Rembrandt shows us a Mennonite preacher famed for his sermons who was also a rich merchant, fond of fine clothes. Seated at his desk, Anslo gestures with his left hand toward a book that seems to emit its own light – his chief inspiration, the Bible. Anslo's right hand, holding a pen, rests atop another book, likely full of his own theological writings. Lips subtly parted, he turns his head to an unseen listener, a gesture through which Rembrandt clearly evokes the act of preaching.

Rembrandt has included in the room what appears to be a painting, taken down from a wonderfully illusionistic nail[1] above Anslo's head, and turned to face the wall. The prevailing interpreta-

---

1 A similar nail appears in the wall behind the sitter in Rembrandt's 1656 portrait of the goldsmith Jan Lutma (White-Boon 276). Curiously, Rembrandt left the nail in the composition even after he changed that area of the wall into a window, leaving the nail hanging in space.

19

tion of this painting's presence in a portrait of a Protestant minister is as an acknowledgment of the Protestant view of the spoken word's supremacy over the visual image. In the contest between the verbal and the visual suggested by Anslo's speaking and the turned-around painting (which Rembrandt signs, to leave no doubt about where he stands), this may be a playful admission by the artist that the word, as spoken by Anslo's voice, wins out in this case.

That the object in the background is a painting at all has come under serious scrutiny.[2] But an irregularly trimmed canvas or panel does seem tacked to the frame with visible nails. And while a frame with a rounded top is unusual in depictions of Dutch domestic interiors, such a shape is more common as a frame for religious images – at least in Rembrandt's own work. First, in his portrait etching of Jan Uytenbogaert of 1639, two years previous, we see a similar if wider picture frame on the wall of Uytenbogaert's office, depicting the Old Testament scene of *Moses and the Brazen Serpent*. Later, in Rembrandt's 1657 etched portrait of the apothecary and art collector Abraham Francen, Rembrandt places a triptych, with a Rembrandt-esque crucifixion scene in its center panel, on the wall of Francen's study.[3] It is identical in its curved top with nail hole to the object in the Anslo portrait. Especially since Anslo is a Christian preacher, it is likely Rembrandt here meant to similarly indicate a religious picture turned to the wall. Through this dismounting of a religious image, Rembrandt strengthens the contrast between the power of Anslo's voice and the power of visual images to convey the word of God.

Much has also been made of the existence of a contemporary poem by the important Dutch poet Joost van den Vondel, praising Anslo's eloquence, that is written onto several extant impressions of the Anslo etching:

Aÿ, Rembrant, mael Cornelis Stem.
Het Zichtbre deel is 't minst van hem:
'tonsichbre kent men slechts door d'ooren.
Wien Anslo zien wil, moet hem hooren.

O, Rembrandt, paint Cornelis' voice.
The visible part is the least of him;
the invisible is known only through the ears;
he who would see Anslo must hear him.[4]

In his epigram, Vondel is teasing Rembrandt about the limitations of his portrait, because Rembrandt cannot literally portray the preacher's greatest attribute, his voice. In so doing, Vondel is taking part in a centuries-old debate between the relative ability of poetry and painting to capture the likeness and spirit of a sitter that goes back to the Italian poet Petrarch (1305–1377). In his sonnet 78, *Quando giunse a Simon l'alto concetto*, Petrarch chides the painter Simone Martini (ca. 1284–1344), a pupil of Giotto, for having masterfully depicted in a portrait drawing everything about Petrarch's beloved Laura except her voice which he so longs to hear.[5]

Whether or not Vondel's verses gave rise to Rembrandt's trick with the dismounted painting, or vice versa, the figure of Anslo also serves as a personification of eloquence based on the *Iconologia* of Cesare Ripa, and therefore makes a strong connection between verbal eloquence and the written word[6] as expressed by the weighty tomes on Anslo's desk. Also, the aforementioned debate between poetry and art gave rise to the Renaissance conceit, still current in Rembrandt's own day, that the ultimate proof of a portrait's illusionistic quality was if it seemed about to speak. Since Rembrandt loved Renaissance portraiture and was undoubtedly familiar with this idea, it is another layer of interpretation that must be present when we look at Anslo's "speaking" likeness. And after all, doesn't Rembrandt get the last laugh by creating a visual vehicle that brings us the duel in which the verbal is supposedly the victor? Even if Rembrandt is turning one picture to the wall, he is doing it by furnishing us another.

A.C.W.

2 Erik Hinterding, et al., *Rembrandt the Printmaker*. London: British Museum, 2000, p. 196.

3 In a sense, the 1657 Francen portrait is the antithesis of the Anslo portrait – it depicts a man who is a firm believer in the communicative power of the visual (as evidenced by the fact that his open book on the table is not a Bible but an album of drawings) and so Rembrandt can safely hang a religious triptych (and other paintings) on his wall.

4 Erik Hinterding, et al., *Rembrandt the Printmaker*, p. 200. The time relationship between the conception of Rembrandt's portrait of Anslo and van den Vondel's composition of the poem is still in question, because the poem did not appear in print until 1644. Translation by Martin Royalton-Kisch.

5 Robert M. Durling trans. and ed., *Petrarch's Lyric Poems, the Rime Sparse and other Lyrics*. Cambridge, MA: Harvard University Press, 1976, p. 178.

6 W. Busch, "Zu Rembrandts Anslo-Radierung," *Oud Holland*, LXXXVI, 1971, pp. 196–197. As cited in Martin Royalton-Kisch, *Drawings by Rembrandt and His Circle in the British Museum*, London: British Museum, 1992, p. 91, n. 5.

20 *The raising of Lazarus: small plate*

1642
Etching and drypoint with burr on cream laid paper.
Bartsch 72; White-Boon 72 i/ii.

PLATEMARK:
151 × 115 mm.

SHEET:
176–177 × 136–135 mm.

INSCRIPTION ON PLATE:
Rembrandt f 1642 (the
2 reversed), at lower left.

PROVENANCE:
Craddock & Barnard,
London, May 5, 1966.

S.W.P.

The story of Lazarus is found in John 11; Lazarus, the brother of Mary Magdalene, has fallen ill and died in their home town of Bethany. Arriving there four days after his death, Jesus commands, against objections that the dead man's corpse will stink, that the stone be removed from his tomb. Jesus cries, "Lazarus, come out!" and Lazarus miraculously emerges, still in his burial wrappings. Lazarus's death and resurrection foreshadow Christ's own, and Rembrandt explores this idea more fully in this second version of the subject, which is a complete departure from the Baroque composition of ten years before in which a dramatically illumined Christ calls Lazarus from the tomb with a powerful gesture of command. This smaller plate is more understated in every way, showing a subtler and more human view of Christ, and a new understanding of the event's significance in the gospel narrative. In this sense, in spite of the many differences, the 1642 Lazarus etching looks back to a painting and an etching by Jan Lievens, Rembrandt's artistic peer during his years in Leiden, a friend and rival with whom he shared ideas.[1] In Lievens's works, Jesus does not gesture to Lazarus, but instead looks heavenward, his hands folded, acting as the conduit for God's will, as Lazarus's pale hands reach astonishingly up out of the grave.

Here, Christ's left hand is raised in a gesture that combines the command to Lazarus with an act of benediction. This should by all means be a right-handed gesture, but typically Rembrandt has not

---

1 Lievens's painting of the Raising of Lazarus, now in the Brighton Museum and Art Gallery, Brighton, England, may be the one listed in the inventory of Rembrandt's possessions in 1656. See Kenneth Clark, *Rembrandt and the Italian Renaissance*. New York: New York University Press, 1964, p. 195.

20

bothered, when sketching on the plate, to account for the composition's reversal when printed. The tilt of Christ's head, downward toward his resurrected friend but also slightly to the side, communicates a thoughtful air, as if Christ is also meditating on this prefiguration of his own death and entombment. Rembrandt never could have seen in his own topographically flat country the rocky wall that frames the composition, or the hill town visible through the opening in the rocks. These are reminiscent instead of Italian landscape, which Rembrandt only knew through works of art – especially prints. Particularly given the similarity of its subject, Rembrandt may have been inspired here by Andrea Mantegna's engraving of the *Entombment*, ca. 1470 (fig. 1), a print Rembrandt admired and probably owned because he made a drawn copy of it.[2] Mantegna's print also features a rocky tomb and a distant hill (Golgotha, where Christ was crucified). Always a transformative borrower, Rembrandt may be invoking Mantegna's *Entombment* to temper the wonder of the Lazarus miracle with a note of sadness, which is appropriate to viewing the scene as a foretelling of Christ's own coming death.

A.C.W.

FIG. I.
Andrea Mantegna
The Entombment, ca. 1465–70
Engraving
Herbert F. Johnson Museum of Art,
Membership Purchase Fund

2 A general sense of the importance of Mantegna's work to Rembrandt is signaled by another entry in the 1656 inventory, which describes "'t Kosselijke boeck van Andre Mantagnie" – "the precious book of Andrea Mantegna" – certainly an album containing his prints. See Clark, *Rembrandt and the Italian Renaissance*, pp. 147 and 202.

2 1 *Self-portrait in a flat cap and embroidered dress*

About 1642
Etching and drypoint with burr on ivory laid paper.
Bartsch 26; Biörklund-Barnard 38 i/ii; Hind 157 i/ii; Nowell-Usticke 26 i/iii; White-Boon 26 only state.

PLATEMARK:
93 × 61.5 mm.

SHEET:
98 × 71 mm.

INSCRIPTION ON PLATE:
Rembrandt f. very faintly at
upper left.

PROVENANCE:
Heneage Finch, 5th Earl of
Aylesford, London (L. 58,
on verso); Captain Gordon
W. Nowell-Usticke, Virgin
Islands, Parke-Bernet sale
no. 2609, New York, Octo-
ber 31 – November 1, 1967,
lot 29.

S.W.P.

This self-portrait, one of over twenty Rembrandt made as etchings alone, shows the artist aged thirty-six. As he often did, Rembrandt here experiments with facial expression: his set jaw, pursed lips, and furrowed brow showing concentration, scrutiny, or perhaps irritation. The tilt of his shoulders and the slight lean of his torso give him a swaggering air; this forward incline is accentuated by the shadow of diagonal hatching strokes across his breast. He seems to emerge from the darkness or lean forward into the light, which may also account for his squinting. As in his *Self-portrait Leaning on a Stone Sill* of 1639 (White-Boon 21), the clothes are intentionally archaizing, the slashed shirt and patterned coat recalling Renaissance portraiture. But unlike the earlier portrait, there is a studied carelessness in the disheveled hair and the beret perched frankly, not rakishly, atop the head, that combines with the facial expression and posture to communicate confidence and even indifference to our gaze.

A.C.W.

21

22 *Girl with a basket*

About 1642
Etching.
Bartsch 356; Biörklund-Barnard 42-3 ii/ii; Hind 195 ii/ii; Münz 95 ii/ii;
Nowell-Usticke 356 ii/ii; Ritman 120 ii/ii; Seidlitz 356 ii/ii; White-Boon 356 ii/ii.

PLATEMARK:
88 × 61 mm.

SHEET:
102 × 75 mm.

INSCRIPTIONS ON PLATE:
none.

INSCRIPTIONS AND
MARKS ON SHEET:
On recto in lower right
corner: *323* [Gersaint catalogue number], in brown
ink. On verso: stamp of S.
W. Pelletier [reddish-brown
ink] (2003.10.6.11).

PROVENANCE:
From an old collection in
the South of France to Paul
Prouté S. A., Paris, catalogue
Géricault, 1990, no. 146;
Pace Prints, New York,
June 1990; Artemis Fine
Arts, Ltd., London; Joseph
R. Ritman, Amsterdam,
1990 (not in Lugt); Artemis
Fine Arts Inc., New York,
October 6, 2003, invoice
#157, #17639-120.

DESCRIPTION:
An excellent, crisp impression in black ink on ivory,
laid paper. With inky plate
edges and light plate tone,
in an unwashed, unpressed
condition with seven fine,
vertical lines in upper right
corner, indicative of an early
impression. Nowell-Usticke
describes this print as RRR⁺
(extremely rare). The drawing in Stockholm, *An Old
and a Young Woman in
Discussion* (Benesch 738) of
about 1642 depicts the girl
in reverse and full figure.

LITERATURE:
*Dessins Estampes Anciennes
du XVIᵉ au XVIIIᵉ Siècle,
estampes des XIXᵉ et XXᵉ
Siècles*. Catalogue *Géricault*.
Paris: Paul Prouté S. A.,
1990, p. 61, no. 146 (illustrated; *Belle épreuve de l'état
définitive après les transfor-
mations dans le visage et le
chapeau*).

*A Collection of Etchings by
Rembrandt Harmensz. van
Rijn (1606–1669) formed by
Joseph R. Ritman*. London:
Artemis and Sotheby's
[1995], no. 120 (illustrated;
*An excellent, crisp impression
of the second state*).

EXHIBITED:
Mees Pierson, The Hague,
The Netherlands,
September – October 1996.

Sotheby's, London,
October 1996.

Sotheby's, New York,
November 1996.

S.W.P.

This light, charming study of a young girl, shown here in an extremely fresh impression with just a hint of plate tone, shows Rembrandt working in the same style as his Haarlem contemporary Adri-aen van Ostade, especially in the open friendly expression and the shadow of the cap cast over the eyes. The torso is a deft interplay of rhythmic hatchings and zigzags, and economical "s" strokes indicate the puckering of fabric on the upper sleeve and the shoulder. The subtle inclusion of a shadow at the left saves the print from appearing formulaic or two-dimensional.

A.C.W.

22

23 *Sheet with two studies:*
a tree, and the upper part of a head of the artist wearing a velvet cap

About 1642
Etching on ivory laid paper with light plate tone and inky plate edges.
Bartsch 372; White-Boon 372 ii/ii.

PLATEMARK:
78 × 68 mm.

SHEET:
85 × 75 mm.

INSCRIPTIONS ON PLATE:
none.

PROVENANCE:
L. Godefroy, Paris (cf. L. 1086); I. De Bruijn, Amsterdam; Craddock & Barnard, London, catalogue 112, no. 109, August 1, 1966.

S.W.P.

This sheet of studies includes a finished study of Rembrandt in his beret, but limited to only one eye, as well as a figure in a landscape, an eye, and flowing hair, all at different angles to each other. This extraordinary image has no pictorial coherence, no consistency of illusion or theme, and yet such is Rembrandt's energy and abundance of invention that we are not bothered by this randomness; in fact, if anything, it enhances our enjoyment of the print. We see here in miniature, as it were, the artist's brilliant redefinition of etching as a way of sketching in public, a revolution that was not built on until Goya and later. For a further discussion of this etching, see Susan Donahue Kuretsky's essay, p. 39.

F.W.R.

23

24 *The hog*

1643
Etching with touches of drypoint.
Bartsch 157; Biörklund-Barnard 43-A ii/iii; Hind 304 i/ii; Münz 265 i/ii;
Nowell-Usticke 157 ii/iii; Seidlitz 157 i/ii; White-Boon 157 i/ii.

PLATEMARK:
144.5 × 185.5–182.5 mm.

SHEET:
172–171 × 203.5–205 mm.

INSCRIPTION ON PLATE:
Rembrandt f. 1643 at
lower right.

INSCRIPTIONS AND
MARKS ON SHEET:
On verso: *no. 211*; stamp
of S. W. Pelletier [reddish-
brown ink] (2000.3.16.6);
stamp of Henry Brodhurst
[black ink]; *L. 1296.*

PROVENANCE:
Henry Brodhurst, Mansfield,
England (Lugt 1296, verso);
Picard Audap Solanet &
Associés, Paris, sale March
16, 2000, lot 211.

DESCRIPTION:
A fine impression of the first
state on ivory, laid paper.
With light plate tone. This
state (Biörklund's first) is
before regularizing the
length of the plate to make
the top and bottom dimen-
sions equal. The last state
has new shading on the
boy's face and the ear flap
of the baby's hat.

LITERATURE:
*Estampes Anciennes et
Modernes.* Paris: Picard
Audap Solanet & Associés.
March 16, 2000, lot 211
(illustrated).

S.W.P.

This remarkable etching of 1643 presents a sow
as a more sympathetic creature than the human
beings around it. The man standing in back is a
pig butcher, indicated by the yoke in his left hand.
What is extraordinary here is the reaction of the
three children, and the mother, to the predicament
of the sow, about to be slaughtered. The grimac-
ing boy makes rude noises with the pig bladder
under his arm, and the dark, rather harsh face of
the youngest child (with its protective headgear),
encouraged by the smiling mother, contrasts with
the gentler features of the sow herself. A second
boy smiles broadly behind the mother.

Again, Rembrandt treats the etching plate as
a sketch pad, leaving most of the sheet empty, a
revolutionary conception of the medium and of
the artifice of illusion.

F.W.R.

24 reduced (85% of actual size)

25 Cottages and farm buildings with a man sketching

About 1641–43
Etching on ivory laid paper.
Bartsch 219; White-Boon 219 only state.

PLATEMARK:
129 × 209 mm.

SHEET:
132 × 211 mm.

INSCRIPTIONS ON PLATE:
none.

PROVENANCE:
Berlin Museum duplicate
(L. 1606, on verso); Count
W. Graf von Lepell (L.
1672, on verso); A. Vasel,
Beierstedt (L. 191, on verso);
Craddock & Barnard,
London, July 25, 1967.

S.W.P.

As an extension of his fascination with depicting country people and those on the fringes of society that appear in his many genre etchings, Rembrandt also recorded numerous farmhouse structures from the environs of Amsterdam, capturing their highly individualistic and expressive personalities. Fully a third of his etched landscapes feature houses like these.[1] Houses convey a strongly human presence even if shown without their inhabitants. And although this house's owners are not present, many details of the print speak about them: the roughly constructed outhouse jutting out at left, the laundry hanging out to dry, and the birds alighting in the dove hatch at the top of the barn, where they will be captured to supplement the family's diet.[2]

Two extant sketches of this same farmhouse in reverse of the print make clear that Rembrandt was drawing an actual structure. Idiosyncrasies like the unusual placement of the chimney also indicate that this is a specific house and not a type.[3] The figure of the artist at lower right seems to be an afterthought, as lines from the foreground track right through him as if they had been there first; the edge of the meadow also cuts through his hat and he is etched more darkly than the rest of the composition.[4] In the scholarship on this print, much has naturally been made of this figure of the artist in relationship to Rembrandt himself; however, it seems less likely a self-portrait and more a stand-in for a general artist, reinforcing the creative act of rendering the house and giving a sense of scale to the view.

A.C.W.

1 Boudewijn Bakker, "Langhuis and Stolp: Rembrandt's Farm Drawings and Prints," in Cynthia P. Schneider, et al., *Rembrandt's Landscapes: Drawings and Prints*. Washington, D. C.: National Gallery of Art, 1990, p. 33.

2 Hilliard T. Goldfarb, *A Humanist Vision: The Adolph Weil, Jr. Collection of Rembrandt Prints*. Hanover, NH: Hood Museum of Art, Dartmouth College, 1988, p. 166.

3 Schneider, *Rembrandt's Landscapes*, p. 85.

4 *Rembrandt Beyond the Brush: Master Prints from the Weil Collection*. Montgomery, Alabama: Montgomery Museum of Fine Arts, 1999, p. 65.

25 reduced (80% of actual size)

26 *The shepherd and his family*

1644
Etching and drypoint with burr on ivory laid paper with plate tone.
Bartsch 220; White-Boon 220 only state.

PLATEMARK:
95 × 67 mm.

SHEET:
96 × 67 mm.

INSCRIPTION ON PLATE:
Rembrandt f. 1644 at
upper left.

PROVENANCE:
Unidentified collector
(initials J.B.O., on verso,
in graphite, not in Lugt);
unidentified collector
(L. 2883a, on verso); Craddock & Barnard, London,
July 9, 1968.

S.W.P.

In this charming but unusual image, Rembrandt seems to mingle genre and religious subjects, crafting a scene of a country couple with their livestock that also has overtones of a *Flight into Egypt* complete with a Madonna and Child and a watchful Joseph. The stone-walled hill town rising in the background, with its suggestion of ancient ruins, is decidedly Italian, so the print cannot be easily classed with Rembrandt's many landscape etchings of the rural environs of Amsterdam. It is also interesting to note that everyone or everything in the print is drinking – the shepherd with his tankard of ale, the child at its mother's breast, and the sheep and goats at the water's edge.

This plate was perhaps reused several times, because Rembrandt's landscape with the family shares the picture space with two large, overlapping circles; either Rembrandt obtained this plate from the publisher of a mathematical or geometric treatise of some kind (as he sometimes did[1]) and reused it without completely cleaning off the pre-existing diagram, or else perhaps the designs were on the other side of the plate and their forms conveyed themselves more or less consciously to Rembrandt as he worked on this image. In any case, it does appear that Rembrandt intentionally caused the silhouette of the hill town to conform to the circle already on the plate, and not vice versa. Also, Rembrandt has added the bushes and tree at the right to cover a grouping of oval forms and several long strokes – tantalizing elements of an aborted image begun with the plate turned horizontally.

A.C.W.

---

1 Ludwig Münz, *Rembrandt's Etchings*, vol. 1.
London: Phaidon Press, p. 11.

26

27 *The hundred guilder print*

About 1643–49
Etching on ivory laid paper.
Bartsch 74; Nowell-Usticke 74, first Baillie retouching; White-Boon 74 ii/ii, Baillie.

PLATEMARK:
279–276 × 398–397 mm.

SHEET:
292–287 × 403 mm.

INSCRIPTIONS ON PLATE:
none.

PROVENANCE:
Craddock & Barnard,
London, December 2, 1968.

S.W.P.

This is a fascinating example of the life of an etching, and, in particular, an etching plate. This impression was not taken by Rembrandt himself, but long after his death, when it had been recut by a later hand. Still later, the plate was even cut into several pieces, with prints taken from each of those pieces.

As S. William Pelletier discusses in his brilliant introductory essay, this famous print brings together several incidents in chapter 19 of the book of Matthew: the old and sick on the right, the children approaching Christ on the left, the rich young man, and the Pharisees on the far left. The basic composition of this work from the 1640s is a variation of the one he used in *The Night Watch* from 1642 and other contemporary works: a procession of figures coming through the arch in a city wall, out of the darkness and into the light, toward a gesturing figure in the center. There is a remarkable variety here, for example, just among the sick; one man walks with a stick, another, with a crutch, kneels on the ground (or perhaps has no legs), one woman is on a fiber mat, another on a bed, and a third on a makeshift wheelbarrow. The line of their hands undulates across the sheet, from right to left, finally casting a shadow of praying hands on Christ's robe. The shell in the right foreground, the symbol of pilgrims, surely refers to the pilgrimage of the lame and the halt above it, while the flowering branch in a slight depression to the left may refer to the children, and the rebirth, and hope, that they represent. As in the artist's 1654 etching of Christ at Emmaus, the three animals – camel, donkey, and dog – turn away from Christ,

27 reduced (40% of actual size)

the central miraculous presence.[1] Christ himself is presented outside the city walls, as an outsider.

Formally, the print is a tour de force of line defining innumerable shapes and textures, and subtle and abrupt transitions from the deepest shadow to bright sunlight. We see here Rembrandt's fascination with clothes of all kinds, and especially hats; there are at least thirty-two hats or head coverings, each one different from the other. The most dramatic is on the left; we see here a brilliant reversal of expectations: the highly detailed, finished hat above, and below, just the outlines of the substantial body that supposedly supports the hat. This "incomplete," sketchlike quality constitutes a remarkable break in the continuity of the etching's pictorial illusion, a surely conscious denial, or manipulation, of our expectations of what a "picture" should be, and one more example of Rembrandt's revolutionary conception of the medium.

We also see here a transitional image in Rembrandt's changing conception of Christ. Earlier, for example, in his etching of the Raising of Lazarus from about 1631–32, Christ is a monumental, commanding figure, the hero. By the 1640s, as in his *Raising of Lazarus* of 1642 (cat. no. 20) and in the "Hundred Guilder Print," he is less dominant, quieter, and by the 1650s, in the *Ecce Homo* or the *Three Crosses*, he is often smaller, humbler, more vulnerable, the victim and hardly the hero. In the *Denial of Peter*, in Amsterdam, from 1660, for example, Christ is barely visible in the background, his hands bound behind him, as he glances over his shoulder at the betrayal.

F.W.R.

---

1 Sympathetic though Rembrandt is to animals (as in the etching of the sow, cat. no. 24), he often shows them unaware of religiously significant events happening around them; sometimes, that lack of awareness takes on a scatological character, as in the defecating dog in the *Good Samaritan* or the dog in *Joseph Telling His Dreams* (cat. no. 18).

27 detail, actual size

1651
Etching and drypoint.
Bartsch 42; Biörklund-Barnard 51-D i/ii; Hind 252 only state; Münz 181 i/ii; Nowell-Usticke 42 i/ii;
Ritman 20 i/ii; Seidlitz 42 only state; White-Boon 42 i/ii.

PLATEMARK:
160 × 126 mm.

SHEET:
191 × 147.5–145 mm.

INSCRIPTIONS ON PLATE:
Rembrandt f. 1651. at lower center; *Rembrandt f 1651* at lower right.

INSCRIPTIONS AND MARKS ON SHEET:
On recto: *To Richard Fisher Esqr. – a print of no value – but certainly / one of the best of Rembrandts works. S. Haden* [brown ink]. On verso: *Joseph R. Ritman / cat. no. 20 (1995)* [graphite]; stamp of S. W. Pelletier [reddish-brown ink] (2000.8.2.9); *Zu 3640* [graphite].

WATERMARK:
Seven Provinces.

PROVENANCE:
Sir Francis Seymour Haden, London (cf. Lugt 1227) presented to Richard Fisher; Richard Fisher, Hill Top, Midhurst, England (cf. Lugt 2204), his sale, London, May 27, 1892, lot 765, £2.10 [Sotheby's] to R. Gutekunst; [Craddock & Barnard, London] sold to [C. G. Boerner, Düsseldorf, September 1958 for £560 less 12%]; [C. G. Boerner, Düsseldorf, 1959, Neue Lagerliste Nr. 24, lot 198]; sold to a private German collector in March 1959; repurchased by C. G. Boerner, Düsseldorf in 1991; sold to Joseph R. Ritman, Amsterdam in 1991; Joseph R. Ritman, Amsterdam (not in Lugt),

FIG. 2.
Jacques Callot, Title Page to *Les Gueux* (Beggars), 1622
Etching
Herbert F. Johnson Museum of Art,
Membership Purchase Fund

Here Rembrandt sets a pivotal scene from the apocryphal book of Tobit, when Tobit's blindness is about to be miraculously cured by the arrival of his son Tobias bearing a magical ointment made from the gall of a fish. Here, he reacts to the news that his son has come home; Rembrandt sets the text, "Tobit went forth toward the door, and he stumbled," quite literally. In his haste in getting up, Tobit overturns a spinning wheel by the hearth and heads straight for the wall, missing the open door completely.

As S. William Pelletier points out in his essay in this catalogue, it was first noted in the nineteenth century by Charles Blanc that the figure of Tobit owes a formal debt to Raphael's tapestry cartoon of *The Blinding of Elymas*, Agostino Veneziano's engraving which Rembrandt probably owned.[1] However, the 1622 beggar etchings of Jacques Callot, *Les Gueux*, which Rembrandt also owned, and which profoundly influenced his many depictions of lower-class Dutch life, were still an important source for this figure of Tobit. Here, Rembrandt copies Tobit's staggering gait, the left foot dragging behind the right, from the staggering old soldier on Callot's title page of the series (fig. 2) – right down to his slippers. This pose is reproduced in reverse in Rembrandt's etching, which shows that Rembrandt drew on his plate in the same orientation as Callot's print. It is certainly no coincidence that Callot's etching also features a blind old man in the background with a skullcap and a cane, being led by a young boy.

The spare interior of Tobit's house is a fairly common depiction of a modest seventeenth-century Dutch interior; indeed the fireplace with

---

1 Charles Blanc, *L'oeuvre complet de Rembrandt décrit et commenté*, Paris, 1859–61, 2 vols, no. 15.

To Richard Fisher Esq — a print of no value — but certainly one of the best of Rembrandts Works.

S. Haden

28

cat. 1995, no. 20; C. G. Boerner Inc., New York, August 2, 2000.

DESCRIPTION:
A beautiful impression of the first state in black ink on thin, off-white, laid paper. The printing is crisp, strong, and particularly effective on the blank wall by the door, where a streak of sulfur tone gives texture. An unusual effect is the strong drypoint under Tobit's feet, which heightens the illusion of his stumbling progress to the door.

LITERATURE:
Catalogue of A Collection of Engravings, Etchings and Woodcuts by Old Masters of the Italian, German, Dutch and other Schools formed by R. Fisher, Esq. Deceased. London: Sotheby, Wilkinson & Hodge, May 27, 1892, lot 765.

Graphik und Handzeichnungen älter und neuer Meister (Neue Lagerliste Nr. 24). Düsseldorf: C. G. Boerner, 1959, lot 198. (illustrated in pl. XIX; *Brillanter Abdruck.... Ein höchst qualifiziertes und einmaliges Exemplar.*)

A Collection of Etchings by Rembrandt Harmensz. van Rijn (1606–1669) formed by Joseph R. Ritman. London: Artemis and Sotheby's [1995], no. 20 (illustrated; *...a beautiful impression of the first state*).

EXHIBITED:
C. G. Boerner, Düsseldorf, March 15 – April 15, 1959.

Mees Pierson, The Hague, The Netherlands, September – October 1996.

Sotheby's, London, October 1996.

Sotheby's New York, November 1996.

S.W.P.

its hood and the placement of the decorative dish above the window at left recall prints of interiors with which Rembrandt would have been familiar, such as Claes Janszoon Visscher's *Family Saying Grace* of 1609 (Hollstein 14), a popular engraving Rembrandt would almost certainly have known. The dish is probably a *plooischotel* or "pleated dish," a hammered silver dish with rounded lobes around the edge.[2] In keeping with Rembrandt's fondness for visual symbols and puns,[3] he underscores Tobit's Job-like patience and humility with a radiating pattern of hatched lines around the edge of the dish, turning it into a halo that hovers above Tobit's head. The posed, theatrical feeling of the scene is reinforced by the edge of the floor, which drops off in imitation of a theatre stage; Rembrandt used a similar effect in his 1654 etching *Christ at Emmaus: the larger plate* (B. 87).

A.C.W.

---

2 Mariët Westermann, *Art & Home: Dutch Interiors in the Age of Rembrandt*, Denver Museum and the Newark Museum, 2001, p. 206–207, cat. nos. 104 and 105.

3 See Franklin W. Robinson, "Puns and Plays in Rembrandt's Etchings," *Print Collector's Newsletter*, vol. II, no. 5 (November – December 1980), pp. 165–168.

29 *Peasant family on the tramp*

About 1652
Etching on cream, laid paper with light plate tone and inky plate edges.
Bartsch 131; White-Boon 131 i/ii.

PLATEMARK:
122 × 92.5 mm.

SHEET:
126 × 97 mm.

INSCRIPTIONS ON PLATE:
none.

PROVENANCE:
Craddock & Barnard,
London, March 2, 1967.

S.W.P.

This is probably the last of Rembrandt's etchings of tramps, from the early 1650s. Somehow, the artist manages to suggest a scene in the country-side, in full sunlight, with this quietly happy family making their way forward. Once again, we see Rembrandt's fascination with clothes as an expression of a person's situation in life; his love of hats is clear in the man's hat, which was drawn once, and then extended. The family is happy: the man holds his son's hand as the son holds the leash of the unseen dog. The mother, with a second, happy child on her back, is barefoot, even though this is not summer, as we see from the boy's coat and the man's many layers of clothing.[1]

Rembrandt's ease of execution and prolific spontaneity resulted in his often making "mistakes" (e.g., giving a second left hand to a figure) or not burnishing out the first versions of his composition, as in the head floating on the right in this print. These remarkable details, which occur so often, may be a product of haste to a great degree, but they also constitute a new conception of etching as a kind of public shorthand, the first thoughts characteristic of a drawing translated into the more public medium of the multiple, etching. In other words, these signs of haste and "incompleteness" in themselves become a part of his artistic personality.

F.W.R.

---

1 Once again, in his 1645 *Rest on the Flight*, the man, Joseph, wears shoes, while the woman, Mary, is barefoot.

29

30 *The circumcision in the stable*

1654
Etching on soft, ivory laid paper with plate tone.
Bartsch 47; Hind 274 i/iii; White-Boon 47 i/ii.

PLATEMARK:
95.5 × 146 mm.

SHEET:
96.5 × 147 mm.

INSCRIPTIONS ON PLATE:
(The d reversed), at upper
left; *Rembrandt f. 1654*, at
center left next to ladder.

PROVENANCE:
Willem Six; sold to Jacob
Houbraken, 1734; to Peter
Cornelis Baron van Leyden,
1739; to Johan Gail, 1788;
Mme. Gail; purchased by
the Rijksmuseum, 1808
(stamp of the Royal Library,
L. 240, on verso); sold by
the Rijksmuseum as a dupli-
cate (Rijksprentenkabinet
duplicate stamp, L. 699, on
verso), May 2, 1882, through
Frederick Muller & Co.;
Craddock & Barnard,
London, December 8, 1967.

S.W.P.

In 1654 Rembrandt executed a series of six small
prints illustrating the childhood of Christ, from
the *Adoration of the Shepherds* to *Christ Returning
from the Temple with His Parents*. The gentleness
and vulnerability that we see in the artist's conception of Christ in the 1650s is clear in this series,
even in the scene of his disputing with the doctors,
where he is sketched in with a minimum number
of strokes.

In the *Circumcision*, the Christ child is the center of loving attention, but he is quiet; he is not
the screaming, squirming infant of Rembrandt's
two earlier versions of the scene, from the 1620s
and early 1630s, both of which take place in the
temple. The unusual placement of this ritual in
the stable in itself expresses the artist's new conception of the humbler, more vulnerable, more
accessible Christ. Interestingly, the stable represented here is quite different from that in the *Adoration of the Shepherds*; Rembrandt is never bound
by that kind of petty consistency. Similarly, he has
signed himself twice, on the left, without bother-
ing to cover over the earlier, less visible signature.

Here, in depicting the first ritual pain of
Christ, the artist inserts a detail reminiscent of
the *Crucifixion and Deposition*, the last ritual pain
of his life: the wooden beam and the ladder leaning against it. As Dorothy Limouze suggests,[1] the
older, frowning woman above the beatific Virgin
may be the prophetess Anna (Luke 2:36), who pre-
dicted Christ's role as redeemer.

F.W.R.

---

1 Dorothy Limouze and Susan Donahue Kuretsky, *The Felix
M. Warburg Print Collection. A Legacy of Discernment*. Vassar
College, 1995, p. 135.

30

31 *Abraham's sacrifice*

1655
Etching with touches of drypoint.
Bartsch 35; Biörklund-Barnard 55-B only state; Hind 283 only state; Münz 184 only state;
Nowell-Usticke 35 only state; Seidlitz 35 only state; White-Boon 35 only state.

PLATEMARK:
157.5 × 133 mm.

SHEET:
194 × 166 mm.

INSCRIPTION ON PLATE:
Rembrandt f 1655. (the *d* and the *6* reversed), in lower right corner.

INSCRIPTIONS AND MARKS ON SHEET:
On verso: *g¹ no 33* [graphite]; stamp of S. W. Pelletier [reddish-brown ink] (2001.3.20.3); *39* [graphite]; *B. 35* [graphite]; *B. 33* [graphite]; *DA* [graphite].

WATERMARK:
Strasbourg Lily (fragment).

PROVENANCE:
Hans Louis Rumbler, Frankfurt am Main (1895–1970); Helmut H. Rumbler, Frankfurt am Main, 2001, Katalog 37, nr. 8.

DESCRIPTION:
A brilliant impression in black ink on ivory, laid paper. With some burr below the angel's right elbow, on the dark patch on Abraham's beard, and on the vertical lines below and to the left of the large basin at the lower center of the print.

LITERATURE:
Rembrandt f (Katalog 37). Frankfurt am Main: Helmut H. Rumbler, March 2001, no. 8 (illustrated).

EXHIBITED:
The European Fine Art Fair. Maastricht, The Netherlands: Helmut H. Rumbler, Booth 360, March 10–18, 2001.

S.W.P.

Rembrandt was fascinated by Abraham and his relationship to his two sons; one, Ishmael, he dismissed into the wilderness, and the other he took to the top of a mountain to sacrifice. Interestingly, Rembrandt's one surviving child, his son Titus, would have been about fourteen years old in 1655, the date of this print.

The three figures are locked together in a pose that is strangely static, given the fact that a father is about to execute his son; the gesture of the angel is a quiet combination of gentleness and strength. In his painting of Jacob Wrestling with the Angel, in Berlin, also from the 1650s, Jacob strains, but the angel, as in the etching, is gentle and loving. In *Abraham's Sacrifice*, Rembrandt has left visible a few changes to the plate; for example, he has moved the platter, to receive the blood, to a more central position, to emphasize its function and strengthen the central axis of the whole composition. As so often in his prints, he has only partly burnished out its previous position to the left. His first placement of the dagger's scabbard was, perhaps, not dramatic enough, so he has inserted a second, larger one. The angel's right hand – such a key detail in the scene – seems to have only four fingers, a "mistake" which, if anything, intensifies the strength of his gesture. Even the sticks of wood at the bottom seem to form the letter "A." As has often been noted, the emotional tenor of this etching is strikingly different from that of his large painting of the same subject, twenty years earlier, in St. Petersburg; in the latter, the High Baroque composition even shows the knife in midair, falling from Abraham's open hand.

Rembrandt is always interested in telling the story, the sequence of events, so he has put in the ram, who will be sacrificed in place of Isaac, under the right wing of the angel, his horns caught in the brambles.

F.W.R.

31

32 *Christ appearing to the apostles*

1656
Etching.
Bartsch 89; Biörklund-Barnard 56-A only state; Hind 237 only state; Münz 220 only state; Nowell-Usticke 89 only state;
Ritman 54 only state; Seidlitz 89 only state; White-Boon 89 only state.

PLATEMARK:
163 × 212 mm.

SHEET:
164 × 214 mm.

INSCRIPTION ON PLATE:
Rembrandt f. 1656 at
lower center.

INSCRIPTIONS AND
MARKS ON SHEET:
On recto: dry stamp of
Prince Nikolaus Esterházy.
On verso: stamp of S. W.
Pelletier [brownish-black
ink] (2003.10.8.13); stamp
of Orazágos Képtár [brown
ink]; stamp of Felix Somary
[violet ink].

WATERMARK:
W.

PROVENANCE:
Prince Nikolaus Esterházy,
Vienna (Lugt 1966, dry
stamp on recto); purchased
by the Hungarian state in
1870 for Országos Képtár
[National Gallery], Budapest
(Lugt 2000, on verso); sale,
Leipzig, May 8–12, 1922,
lot 888 [C. G. Boerner], to
Guiot for 100,000 marks;
Gilhofer and Ranschburg,
Lucerne, sale to Felix
Somary, Zürich and Wash-
ington, D. C. (not in Lugt),
June 1938; Artemis Fine
Arts Ltd., London and N.
G. Stogdon, Inc., New York
[from catalogue of Felix
Somary prints, 1985], sale
to Joseph R. Ritman, Ams-
terdam (not in Lugt), July
1987; Artemis Fine Arts Inc.,
New York, October 8, 2003,
invoice #158, #17639-54.

DESCRIPTION:
A very fine, early, crisp
impression in black ink on
ivory, laid paper, with light
plate tone, inky plate edges
and square plate corners.

There is only slight blurred
printing along the left edge
of the print. Later, less crisp
impressions show clear double printing along the left
edge. Nowell-Usticke says,
"*Most impression* [sic] *are
slipt in the printing & rather
blurred at the L.*" J. P. Filedt
Kok states, "*Most good
impressions of B. 89.... are
somewhat fuzzy in the lower
left, probably because Rembrandt ran them through the
press twice* (K. G. Boon, oral
communication)." Nowell-
Usticke describes this print
as RRRR ("*a great rarity*").
    This print is generally
interpreted either as an illustration of John 20:19-23,
when Christ made his first
appearance to his disciples
after his resurrection or of
John 20:24-29, when he
appeared a second time eight
days later and removed
Thomas's doubts as to his
resurrection. Christopher
White favors the first
appearance and identifies
the kneeling figure as Peter,
while J. P. Filedt Kok favors
the second appearance and
identifies the kneeling figure as Thomas.

LITERATURE:
*Kupferstichsammlung Dr.
Julius Hofmann Wien. Dabei
Doubletten eines bedeutenden
stattlichen Kupferstichkabinetts*
[Budapest duplicates].
Leipzig: C. G. Boerner, May
8–12, 1922, lot 888 (illustrated in pl. 28; *Das genial
radierte Blatt in ausgezeich-
netem Abdruck, mit Plattenton
und gratigen Rändern*).

*Etchings by Rembrandt from
the Collection of Felix Somary.*
London: Artemis Fine Arts
(UK) Limited and New
York: N. G. Stogdon, Inc.

As Hans-Martin Rotermund has shown, Rembrandt used different haloes for different stages in
the life of Christ. In this posthumous appearance
to seventeen or eighteen of his followers, with
Peter or Thomas kneeling in front of him, the
light from his halo almost blinds them, and they
turn away from it; they, and the figure of Christ
himself, are virtually dematerialized by the waves
of unearthly light. Only the barest outlines and
simplest details are sketched in, and even the
magisterial central figure is weightless, standing
on clouds, almost transparent, dissolved in his own
halo. To give some kind of anchor to the composition, the artist has placed a solid, heavy chair on
the left edge, with a heavyset man sitting next to
it, and a simple bench on the far right. The arrangement of the standing Christ surrounded by kneeling and standing figures is familiar to us from
other prints of the 1640s and 1650s, such as the
"Hundred Guilder Print" (cat. no. 27) and *Christ
Preaching ("La Petite Tombe")*.

F.W.R.

[1985], no. 24 (illustrated;
A fine impression).

*A Collection of Etchings by
Rembrandt Harmensz. van
Rijn (1606–1669) formed by
Joseph R. Ritman.* London:
Artemis and Sotheby's
[1995], no. 54 (illustrated;
*An unusually fine impression
of an exceptionally rare plate,
with a lightly controlled ink
tone, but without the "double
printing" often found in the
left-half*).

EXHIBITED:
Mees Pierson, The Hague,
September – October 1996.

Sotheby's, London,
October 1996.

Sotheby's, London,
November 1996.

S.W.P.

32

Clifford S. Ackley. *Printmaking in the Age of Rembrandt*. Boston: Museum of Fine Arts, 1981.

Clifford S. Ackley, Ronni Baer, Thomas E. Rassieur, and William W. Robinson. *Rembrandt's Journey: Painter, Draftsman, Etcher*. Boston: Museum of Fine Arts, 2003.

Holm Bevers, Peter Schatborn, and Barbara Welzel. *Rembrandt: The Master & His Workshop, Drawings and Etchings*. New Haven: Yale University Press, 1991.

Kenneth Clark. *Rembrandt and the Italian Renaissance*. New York: New York University Press, 1964.

Erik Hinterding, Ger Luijten, and Martin Royalton-Kisch. *Rembrandt the Printmaker*. London: British Museum, 2000.

Martin Royalton-Kisch. *Drawings by Rembrandt and His Circle in the British Museum*. London: British Museum, 1992.

Cynthia P. Schneider, et al. *Rembrandt's Landscapes: Drawings and Prints*. Washington, D.C.: National Gallery of Art, 1990.

Mariët Westermann, et al. *Art & Home: Dutch Interiors in the Age of Rembrandt*, Denver Museum and the Newark Museum, 2001.

Christopher White. *Rembrandt as an Etcher*. New Haven: Yale University Press, 1999.

Christopher White and Karel G. Boon. *Rembrandt's Etchings: An Illustrated Critical Catalogue*. Amsterdam: Van Gendt & Co., 1969, 2 vols.

Julia Lloyd Williams, et al. *Rembrandt's Women*. Edinburgh: National Gallery of Scotland, 2001.

This book was designed and set in type by
Gilbert Design Associates, Providence, Rhode Island.

It was printed by Brodock Press, Inc.
on Garda Silk Cover and Text paper
and bound at The Riverside Group.

The typeface is Janson, a design based on fonts
cut by Miklós Kis, Amsterdam, about 1685.

2000 copies
on the occasion of the exhibition
January 2004